DECORATING
FOR COMFORT

DECORATING

FOR COMFORT

THE MARRIAGE OF EASE AND STYLE

Teri Seidman

& Sherry Suib Cohen

VILLARD BOOKS

NEW YORK • 1995

Original photographs by Bill Rothschild

Library of Congress Cataloging-in-Publication Data
Seidman, Teri.
　　Pure Comfort : decorating for ease and style / by Teri Seidman and Sherry Suib Cohen.
　　　p.　　cm.
　　ISBN 0-679-41838-5
　　1. Interior decoration—Psychological aspects.　I. Cohen, Sherry Suib.　II. Title.
NK2113.S45　1995
747'.1—dc20　　94-15541

Manufactured in the United States of America on acid-free paper

9　8　7　6　5　4　3　2

First Edition

BOOK DESIGN BY BARBARA MARKS

DEDICATED TO OUR AGENT,

THE IRREPRESSIBLE

CONNIE CLAUSEN,

WHO IS THE BEST.

THAT'S ALL—JUST THE BEST.

CONTENTS

Acknowledgments   X

Prologue   XI

I: THE FSC FORMULA   3

II: WHAT'S YOUR DESIGN UMBRELLA?   17

III: VOLUPTUOUS COMFORT   25

IV: SOCIAL COMFORT   59

V:	HIGH-FUNCTION COMFORT	95
VI:	COZY COMFORT	135
VII:	FEATHERING YOUR NEST	161
	Epilogue: The Onion Theory	179
	Resource Guide	181

ACKNOWLEDGMENTS

With the greatest appreciation for his outstanding photography, we thank the amazing Bill Rothschild. His artistry is matched only by his patience and generosity.

Mike Strohl has been terrific—unflaggingly creative and dependable. His contacts with the premier designers in the country have been an invaluable resource.

Diane Reverand is the quintessential editor, the editor of everyone's dreams. As always, she's been brilliant and inventive. Also funny.

With grace and cool, Hilary Black, assistant to Diane Reverand, helped shepherd this book through and we're indebted to her.

Victoria Ceruti and Sally Gilhooley provided cheerful and professional backbone. Our thanks.

A special thanks to the gifted staff at Villard Books—in the departments of design: Victoria Wong and Barbara Marks; production: Filomena Boniello; and copyediting: Martha Schwartz and Sonia Greenbaum.

Finally, we acknowledge our families, Kitty, Larry, Jane, David, Susan, Adam, Jennifer, and Steven, who taught us everything we need to know about the spirit of comfort.

PROLOGUE

The young architect stumbled in the front door, kicked off her expensive shoes, and collapsed into her *beloved* wing chair with a deep sigh. Home again.

The day had been impossible, filled with the exhilaration, but also the stress, of achievement. Her back hurt from hours spent in the chic discomfort of someone else's conference room, her feet ached, and her imagination was stifled. She needed her own richly nurturing surroundings, which greeted her like a hug. At last, she could decompress—draw the shades, plump the pillows, and burrow in with a profound sense of soul-satisfying comfort. The architect gazed with pleasure at the easy elegance that surrounded her and congratulated herself on having turned down an invitation to go out that evening.

All she really wanted was to be home.

HOME AGAIN

The young architect is not alone. In unprecedented numbers, Americans disenchanted with excesses—the overspending, overeating, and overdoing of the last decade—are going home again. Disgusted with marketplace pressure, more and more people are even starting home-based businesses, and part- and full-time home offices are commonplace.

The baby boomers, who traditionally reflect the marketplace, are approaching middle age. This sobering fact is encouraging them to search for the pleasures of home and a more solid life than a free-loving, free-spending existence.

The newest baby boom (in 1991, 4.1 million babies were born—a net increase of 11 percent over the previous four years) suggests that all those new parents out there are becoming home-involved by circumstance as well as by choice. A depressed economy, increased urban crime rates, and frightening AIDS statistics all point to the safety of home and family.

*Home again . . . for
pure comfort.*
Design by Anthony Antine;
photography by Bill Rothschild.

The proof's there: The explosion of VCR sales, take-out foods, and microwave popcorn all indicate an increasingly worn path to the comforts of home.

The lifestyle trend analyst Faith Popcorn gave the phenomenon a name. She called it "cocooning" and described it as a new sort of hypernesting, an impulse to *dig in* and burrow down.

"We're hunkering down, we're holing up, we're hiding out under the covers . . . we're home," wrote Popcorn.

BUT WE'RE NOT HIDING OUT

Faith Popcorn was wrong about one thing: We may be going home again, but we're *not* hiding out. It is true that our habits have changed. Instead of impersonal dining at expensive hot spots that marked the social climbing and networking of the eighties, we're inviting our pals and our colleagues home. Instead of trendy glitz, we're substituting intimate comfort at our own elegant dinner parties.

Instead of the endless search for ways to entertain the children in town, we're opting for games, books, and hobbies we can share with them in activity-rich rooms at home. Comfortable activity rooms help to cultivate sound family values and encourage togetherness. Mom goes over the company report, Dad tends his orchids, the kids are hot into video games, and dinner for all is perking away in a programmed microwave oven.

Conversation has come back, too: Stretching out to chat on a body-embracing sofa in front of the fire suddenly seems more appealing than perching on a bar stool in a noisy, public place.

Home theater has become the entertainment mode of the nineties. Alone or with friends, watching the Big Screen in our own media rooms and not in impersonal movie theaters has become de rigueur. Snug in our nests, we watch blockbuster movies, comedy club routines, and the televised acrobatics of political campaigns.

We're also spending more quiet, introspective time at home. Overdecorated rooms have given way to relaxed spaces that are sometimes romantic, sometimes cozy, sometimes inspiring, and often just comfortable places to dream.

No longer just a place to unwind, home has also become the place for intellectually stimulating, energizing activity. Even the push for physical fitness no longer has to be accommodated at expensive or inconvenient health clubs. More and more of us are working out on treadmills and stair steppers, lifting weights, and luxuriating in saunas in the comfort of home—in the company of friends and family, if we choose.

By going home, we are not seeking isolation. It's simply that we're now doing at home what we used to do outside and we want to be comfortable doing it.

An ancient definition of comfort is *to strengthen.* Decorating with comfort in mind turns the home into a place of ease, but more important, a place of strengthening, because it makes an active life a convenient one.

TO EACH HIS OWN

Comfort means different things to different people.

Walk into your best friend's dimly lit study and sink into her favorite frayed easy chair. You may feel only a sense of gloom and *dis*comfort.

Walk into my office and you'll see me working at my desk, seated on a hand-painted sixteenth-century parlor chair. Sitting in that chair, I feel surrounded by an aura of well-being and beauty. The chair's lineage and its artistry evoke for me a sense of history and a comforting sense of my own endurance. Although the chair may look delicate, it is my safe place.

To my coauthor, Sherry, the chair is torture, not comfort. In her office, she sticks with state-of-the art machinery, Formica and brushed steel. Her word processor is within easy reach of her copier, which is an arm's reach from the work stations where she spreads out her research materials, a rolling chair's roll away from the leather couch on which she hourly needs to rest her back as she reads her work. This small but well-planned office represents quintessential comfort to her.

To each his own.

Sometimes the difficulty in decorating for comfort is trying to figure out what *is* your own. Do you really think you'd love to live with your sister-in-law's wonderfully interesting clutter—or is it just that it seems to complement her lifestyle so perfectly?

Is it most important to you that a room functions well—or is it most important that it feels cozy? Can it do both of these things? Of course it can do both. On one level, comfort is about physical snugness, but on another level, comfort is very much about convenience and ease of activity.

HOME IS NOT A STAGE SET

Years ago, I was involved in theater, and I remember gazing enviously at a magnificent stage set and thinking, "Wouldn't it be something to live in that?" Now, older and wiser, I know that many of the grand salons and the museum-perfect, look-at-me dining rooms of the rich and the famous work wonderfully well for stilted theatrical performances but they fail abysmally as comfortable living spaces. Nobody can live, love, or really relax in a stage set.

In contrast, once I was a dinner guest at the home of the celebrated Paley family. I learned a lesson about comfort that evening. I sipped coffee in a room in which hung a Blue Period Picasso; because the room was so cozy, I never thought about the importance of the picture. I was surrounded by centuries-old furniture of inestimable value, yet I never felt intimidated. Like great hosts, rooms decorated with comfort in mind put you at your ease.

Without comfort, you may go home to your beautifully decorated rooms but you won't feel like staying.

ENTER PURE COMFORT

This book will teach you how to decorate your home so you'll hate to leave it—so *everyone* will hate to leave it. Step by step, I'll show you how to create rooms that look splendid and feel wonderful. The sense of what's right in our homes derives more and more from what feels good: As you read, you'll begin to recognize then trust your own good instincts—the ones that say "This is heaven!"

Two things we must know about comfort:

Comfort is compatible with beauty, style, and elegance. Reject the myth that says comfortable means sloppy.

Comfort does not only involve physical ease and how you feel in a chair. The elements of comfort include functional, emotional, and visual ease. Personal and family well-being are important factors, but so is assuring your friends' comfort when they visit. Comfort is energizing because when we pay attention to comfort, we make it easier to work and play.

Decorating for Comfort has been divided into *four* basic comfort signatures that embrace all the rooms in your home.

Voluptuous Comfort
Social Comfort
High-Function Comfort
Cozy Comfort

Voluptuous Comfort is expressed most beautifully by the sensuality of texture, visual delights, and color. It's a feet-up, hedonistic style. Most of us cherish voluptuous comfort in our bedrooms. Naturally, you may wish to decorate other rooms in your home with voluptuous comfort, and you can take your cues from the ideas in this chapter.

Social Comfort will be of particular interest to those who enjoy the warming moments spent with friends or family. In this section, we look closely at conversational and entertaining ease in our living and dining rooms as well as the warm, welcoming entranceways that are the focal points of social comfort.

High-Function Comfort is crucial in the kitchens, bathrooms, offices, media rooms, and closets in our homes, where ease of function is the first priority. In these rooms, everything must work—*then* look like a dream.

Cozy Comfort is for those who delight in safe, snug, warm places . . . breakfast nooks, garden sanctuaries, window-seat niches, cocktail or coffee retreats. When children find sanctuary in their rooms and as children and adults gather together in common rooms, it's cozy comfort they seek.

The good news is that *Voluptuous, Social, High-Function,* and *Cozy Comfort* are versatile. They can be defined in many decorating styles from Fine Traditional to Classic Americana, from Sleek Contemporary to Tranquil Country, even with a charming Regional Flair—if that's where your heart lies—and you'll find tips for doing that throughout these pages.

In each chapter, there are *Comfort Zone checklists* to help you delineate the obvious as well as the hidden functions of each room. As you define the comfort zone for each room, you'll come to spot potential problems and find solutions before those trouble areas become uncomfortable.

The *FSC Formula (Function, Style, and Comfort)* will help you plan each of the rooms in your home; a *quiz* in the chapter called "What's Your Design Umbrella?" will help you choose the perfect decorating style for your individual taste.

In "Feathering Your Nest," you'll learn how to unify fabric, color, and wall and floor textures. You'll see how to display your art and other treasures to their best advantage. We'll look at how lighting, heating, and cooling are prime requisites of comfort.

You'll learn about plump furniture, sure, but also about a definition of comfort that is broader, more sensible, more demanding. This sense of comfort helps to make your home effortlessly functional so it becomes a place where you can work, exercise, or play efficiently and comfortably. This idea of elegant and functional comfort makes life easier for everyone—and makes a home unique.

Throughout the book, you'll discover how to create relaxed seating arrangements so that your guests can dine and talk with one another without strain. You'll find out how to create delightful personal oases. You'll discover furniture for sinking into, for slumping in, for sheltering and protecting you with a flexible, lovely ease. You'll learn ways to achieve compact comfort in smaller apartments or homes (even your second home should be comfortable) using some clever techniques that make less seem like more. You'll learn how to decorate so that movement within your home is graceful and functional.

In every chapter, you'll find tips on storage. New studies show that busy Americans have less time and even less inclination for keeping houses spotlessly polished à la June Cleaver, so now more than ever we need effortless storage. "People get depressed when they can't see out their windows," says Martha Stewart, the home design doyenne. They get even more depressed when they trip over their shoes or can't find the vegetable peeler. It's not so much housekeeping that's on our minds these days as it is homekeeping—keeping our homes filled with ease and tranquillity.

Finally, you'll find a Resource Guide, which will give suggestions where you can buy the accoutrements of comfort for your own extraordinary home.

Lean back and relax: I'll take you to a nice, comfy place.

DECORATING
FOR COMFORT

A *sunny, country dining corner. Function and style merge for easygoing comfort.*

Design by Mark A. Polo for M.A. Inc., Fort Lee, NJ; photography by Bill Rothschild.

1

THE FSC FORMULA:

FUNCTION, STYLE, AND COMFORT

Before we think about comfort and how our home feels, we must first decide what we want our rooms to do and, roughly, how we want them to look.

The formula for comfort decorating can be reduced to FSC. Think FSC.
Function: establish the function of a room
Style: determine the style of the room
Comfort: plan for the comfort of the room

FUNCTION: WHAT WILL MY ROOM DO?

Classically, the prime purpose of the bedroom is for sleep, but when decorating for comfort, we must rewrite the classics. What else do you do in your bedroom? Do you eat in there when you're too exhausted to set the dining room table? Do you watch television in your bedroom, entertain, work, dress, or dream in there? At the beginning of each chapter, you will find Comfort Zone checklists to help you determine the many functions of each room.

STYLE: HOW WILL MY ROOM LOOK?

The traditional purpose of decorating is to make every room in your home look wonderful by making conscious decisions about its style.

There are many style choices, from country to contemporary, from European elegance to Far Eastern purity. There is an embarrassment of riches to choose from when setting the design tone of your home. The joy of decorating for comfort is in understanding that all of these looks can mark a place where you feel calm and safe.

There is only one rule: Decorating for comfort means *not* being bound by tyrannical rules. Remember to express your own dreams and eccentricities. You can do anything you want, like building your bedroom around a treasured childhood train set or an antique ventriloquist's dummy, instead of sticking with the sterile idea of style that might impress your neighbors. Then, choose a reasonably strong, pull-it-together design umbrella before you select colors, fabrics, and furniture. Here's how to clarify the look you love.

What style makes you happy? Here are some ideas.

Classic Americana: Relax in a heritage-rich, hearth-warmed corner, replete with an American eagle, tufted leather chair, and an English mahogany highboy.

Design by Clark LeCuyer Interior Design; photography by Bill Rothschild.

CLASSIC AMERICANA

This is a look enhanced by grandfather clocks, fine Windsor chairs, and framed needlework. Pewter flagons, three-branched brass candlesticks, copper tableware, and other burnished metalwork abound. Ceramics are ubiquitous—delft, stoneware, and Staffordshire pottery. Glass collections add color and light.

Wonderful woods, such as walnut or curly maple, with mahogany inlays, are used in floor materials, furniture, and on walls. Turkish, Persian, and Chinese rugs, English loomed carpets and American hooked rugs cover many of the wooden floors.

Piecrust tea tables, camelback sofas, wing chairs, sterling silver tea services, and the occasional imposing American eagle punctuate the atmosphere.

Classic Americana design umbrellas feature scenes of triumphant English or American battles on printed fabrics and wallpaper. Window hangings, upholstery, and odd pieces are made of brocades, damasks, toiles, and chintzes as well as the earthier homespun wools and linens.

Traditional accent colors include oxblood reds, deep golds, jade, and classic navy or delft blue shades (never pastels) against backgrounds of muted mustards, blue and white, or light cocoas.

Some people imbue Classic Americana with a Victorian accent—which means armloads of *stuff:* accessories, plants, ceramics, Turkish or Moorish beaded or button-tufted pillows, plants, or Indian artifacts.

The overall effect? Handsome and historical.

Fine Traditional: Ornate fabrics, fringes, and intricate moldings create a lush place to read, dream, and have a cup of tea.

Design by Patricia Sayers at Mansions & Millionaires; photography by Oleg March.

FINE TRADITIONAL

Fine Traditional relies heavily on European accents like ancestor portraits, dog or horse paintings, "puddling" draperies, and tassels, tassels, tassels.

Furniture styles range from Empire, Palladian, Renaissance to all the Looeys—Louis XIV, Louis XV, Louis XVI. Canopied beds, curvy silhouettes, fringes, polished patinas, and pattern-on-pattern decor are typical.

Silks, satins, and brocades are imperative. Lush velvet or ornate needlework cushions soften seating areas.

Gilded moldings and other architectural details are prevalent over doors and mantelpieces, along chair rails, and on the ceiling. Great reproductions are available in any lumberyard.

Golden and crystal candelabra, elaborate picture frames, skirted tables, paneled Chinese screens, sterling silver, and embroidered cushions add an ornate sense of detail.

Fine Traditional color schemes reflect the flavor of the country most heavily represented. For example, the Italian Tuscany area is defined by the burnt siennas, Titian reds, and mellow golds of the area. The jewel tones of a French music box—topaz, rose quartz, pearly gray, and marine blue—might be a color scheme for a home that takes its cues from nineteenth-century Paris.

The overall effect? Lush, abundant, and rich.

Sleek Contemporary: a soothing place— monochromatic wool covers geometric seating. The uncluttered tranquillity provides sophisticated comfort.

Design by Teri Seidman Interiors; photography by Bill Rothschild.

SLEEK CONTEMPORARY

No curvy lines here: Smooth, geometric, unbroken, linear effects and built-in furniture combine with the classic designs of Le Corbusier, Saarinen, and other master designers of the current century to create an uncluttered and clean environment.

Sleek Contemporary takes advantage of the fluid lines of glass and steel, recessed lighting, monochromatic color, and geometric or uniformly rounded shapes. Abstract sculpture and architectural drawings complement the total look.

One color usually dominates: Neutrals like gray, beige, greige, taupe, off-white, or gray-greens are relieved by dashes of color in art, greenery, and accessories.

Remember that less is more, and not every space needs to be filled.

Fabrics are supple and luxurious if you buy the finest: Nubby wools, buttery leathers, sensual velours, and natural cottons and canvases work best.

Elegant lighting is key. Avoid bulky shades, ornate crystal bases, and heavy switch plates. Instead, use recessed or track lighting or long-necked Italian-style lamps or torchères in black or anodized satin-finished silver-tonic metal as simple spot lighting.

The overall effect? Power-stunning; smooth calm.

*Tranquil Country:
informal pleasures
around a potbellied
stove. Handmade
quilts, wicker, and
delicate florals
invite calm.*

Design by Ronald Bricke &
Associates, Inc.;
photography by Michael
Hill.

TRANQUIL COUNTRY

This is a charming, eclectic, quilty, baskety, wickery, folk arty, handmade look!

Country embodies quintessential comfort, often with accents indigenous to its location:

Farmland Tranquil Country is heavy with antique weather vanes, wooden animals, Shaker furniture, and Early American samplers. Seaside Tranquil Country might include antique reed baskets filled with sea glass, white wicker rockers, tea caddies, and plant stands. American Tranquil Country is twig furniture, chintz and calico cottons, organdy curtains, and small-scale prints. French Tranquil Country is inspired by the rich colors of Provence—hand-painted blue-and-white floor tiles, tin-lantern grays, chick-yellow accents, and the reds the color of fine burgundies.

In all aspects of country decorating, make generous use of *prints*—from large-scale florals to delicate miniprints bursting in colorful blooms, tavern tablecloth checks, regimented dots, and trellis patterns on walls, fabrics, and floors. Country reads homemade; it's a look of warmth, combining native art with a sink-in delight.

Any type of collection is country:

- blue willow English china in an antique English hutch
- boxes and baskets in kitchens, halls, bedrooms
- enamelware on a turn-of-the-century stove

The overall effect? Intimate, with an appreciation for simple, unpretentious objects.

REGIONAL FLAIR

Sometimes the area from which one hails (or just loves) suggests a strong design umbrella.

If you live in the Southwest in a pueblo-style home, colors should be indigenous to the land—the cocoa earth, turquoise skies, desert grays, or cactus greens of your environment. Your woody furniture may be handcrafted, and accents of hammered silver, Navajo weavings, and adobe textures can provide visual comfort.

If your home is high in the Adirondacks, your inspiration may come from the mountains and clear skies that also inspire the designer Ralph Lauren. Animal-patterned fabrics, leathers, stone fireplaces, and boldly patterned throw rugs are de rigueur.

Even if you live in the center of New York City, you may be entranced by the tranquillity of a Kyoto inn. Cool, spare, and harmonious grace notes such as lacquered furniture, varied floor levels, shoji screens, and the meditative colors of wood, clay, and hearth will take center stage. Garden stools, antique pillows made from "obis," bamboo screens, three-level simple floral decorations, porcelains, and paper will be hallmarks.

Look around at the sea, desert, hills, plains, or countries that feel like your natural landscape—and create a design umbrella that seems appropriate.

The overall effect? Charming "rightness" and wit.

1. **Time frame (period):** nineteenth century

2. **Place (where style originates):** French Traditional

3. **Formality (casual or formal?):** formal

4. **Colors:** ivory, pale blue, soft rose, antique faded florals

5. **Fabrics/materials:** silk, satin, crushed velvet, needlepoint, deep fringes, Aubusson silk rug, brocades, ornately carved moldings and mantel

6. **Furnishings:** tiered table with ormolu trim; period chest; gilded mirror; bronze sconces; topiaries; porcelain; tufted, upholstered chairs; ancestor portraits

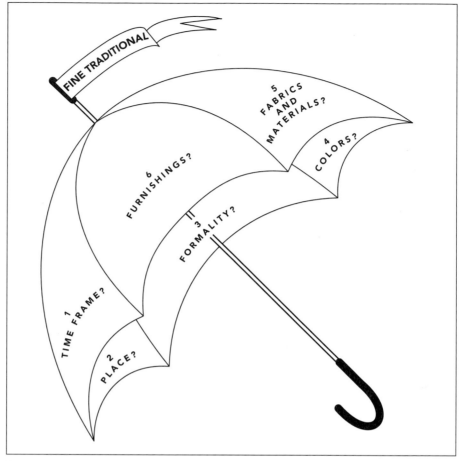

Design umbrella. Illustration by Dani Antiman.

GET A HANDLE ON YOUR DESIGN UMBRELLA

After you settle on a style that makes you happy, think of that look as a design umbrella. The overall sheltering cover is the style, and what fits under the umbrella supports its beauty and energy. Just as an umbrella needs strengthening spokes, every design umbrella needs spokes to clarify its look. The spokes for a design umbrella consist of these elements:

Time Frame: If you opt for a Fine Traditional design umbrella, will it be mostly eighteenth-century traditional or turn-of-the-century traditional? If you opt for a Sleek Contemporary design umbrella, will it be mostly thirties Art Deco contemporary or ninetics contemporary?

Place: Approximately *where* does your style originate? Is it French or English traditional? Is it Italian or American contemporary?

Formality: Are you looking for a casual or formal version of the look?

Color: The rich reds of French eighteenth-century traditional furniture will not be enhanced by a pastel rug. The greige, monochromatic color scheme that works so well for a contemporary look will be diluted with the addition of blue plaid wallpaper, a color touch that might fit under a Tranquil Country umbrella.

Fabrics/Materials: Will gauzy cotton curtains weaken the look? What about heavy brocades? Cotton chintzes or elegant silks? Woods or wrought iron?

Furnishings: Do you prefer modular, or sectional, couches, built-ins, or club chairs? And what about accessories? What will serve the design umbrella best—a collection of ornate silver picture frames or a single crystal obelisk on a glass table?

Remember that each spoke of the design umbrella supports the character of the room. If you completely leave out one or two spokes, the structure is weakened and may even collapse.

AN 80/20 MIX

Although it's important to develop a strong design umbrella, rooms that look as if they belong in museums are not comfortable. Stick *reasonably* to the appropriate elements that support the look. A look is not weakened if there are a few eclectic design surprises to stimulate the eye and lend originality. You can safely depend on an 80/20 mix. If your living room's design umbrella is 80 percent Tranquil Country with the chintzes, baskets, quilts, and French folk art that classically define the look, you can introduce 20 percent from other styles. For example, in such a charming room, recessed lighting from Sleek Contemporary could work very well. A strong design umbrella has a controlling ambience: Either a room is predominantely French Country or North Woods Adirondacks. It can't combine an equal amount of both and still look coordinated or feel peaceful.

What if the controlling style changes from room to room? Try to retain the 80/20 mix for each room. If, for example, your bedroom is decorated under a Tranquil Country design umbrella and your kitchen is strictly sleek contemporary, be consistent within each room.

Naturally, you don't have to decide every detail before you start. Still, an approximate design umbrella for each room you're working on is an intelligent tool for coordinated decorating. Study the sample design umbrella on page 10 to understand how its spokes hold up the overall style of the room.

What if you have no idea which design umbrella to choose?

First, do some easy research.

Begin with creating picture folders. Label legal-sized envelopes COLOR FOLDER, BEDROOM FOLDER, ACCESSORIES FOLDER, FABRIC FOLDER, and start collecting magazine pictures, bits of fabric, and swatches of color that have caught your eye. You'll get real clues as to the broad classifications, time frames, degree of formality, and color schemes to which you're most drawn. You'll spot patterns in the items you've chosen.

For example, if you find yourself clipping out versions of the same damask sofa, the same Victorian-style chaise, the same ancestor pictures, the same coffee table laden with sterling silver frames, the same fringed and tapestried skirted tables, it's a safe bet that the look you love is captured in a nineteenth-century, opulently Victorian, Fine Traditional design umbrella.

Then, find inspiration in the model rooms of department stores, on television programs, and even in museums. Although you don't want a home to be as stiff and staid as a museum exhibition, you'll still find invaluable and surprising design ideas in these rooms.

Keep your design umbrella reasonably *appropriate*. While a Far Eastern influence can look smashing in a living room in a city that's very far from the Far East, somehow an adobe hearth in a Manhattan apartment complex is not really an appropriate style. It seems so out of context, it could look silly.

But if your home is in the great Southwest—do run with that adobe treatment! Make it a perfect adobe hearth using sandstone and wood instead of marble and mahogany, hand-painted tiles instead of brass around the kiva-style fireplace. Accessories should also contribute to the adobe hearth look; the flooring, the furniture, the colors should all support the design umbrella. If you inject tassels and velvet, you'll demolish the style.

Naturally, you can include some touches that are not southwestern, but a style must be clearly stated before it can tolerate other-flavor surprises. Too many flavors create the mishmash look.

When you finish your research, take the quiz in chapter II: It will help you even more clearly define the look you love.

COMFORT: HOW WILL MY HOME FEEL?

Once you've settled on the function and style of the rooms in your home, you are finally ready to turn your thoughts to decorating for comfort—thus completing the FSC formula.

Comfort depends on choosing the furniture you need and allowing for room to move around it gracefully. To do this properly, you must have a floor plan for each room in your home. *Don't skip this step.* No professional would think of decorating a room without first drawing up a floor plan for comfort. Here's how to do it using a living room as an example.

A LIVING-ROOM FLOOR PLAN

You don't have to be an artist or architect to get a visual idea of the approximate scale, placement, and design of the furniture you'll need in each room. Think you want a desk somewhere in this room? Put it on paper. Think you want a small table and chairs for informal brunches with guests? Put it on paper. Nothing you place in this floor plan is engraved in stone. In fact, after you create an approximate drawing of your living room, you may see that your true priorities are revealed: If you simply don't have the space, you may have to choose between the desk and the small table.

This is what you need to make a floor plan:

- tape measure to get the dimensions of the room to be decorated
- ruler to scale your room down to inches on paper
- fine-point black marker and a fine-point colored marker
- sheet of colored poster paper
- scissors
- large piece of white or graph paper

Measure the dimensions of your living room, including all alcoves, and, with the black marker, outline the room on the white (or graph) paper, using a scale of 1 inch equals 1 foot.

With the colored marker, indicate closets, radiators, built-in bookcases, fireplaces, windows, electrical outlets, doors, and architectural elements in the room around which you must decorate. You may have the space in actual footage for the desk, but you have to look at the room in *available* space since the desk can't be placed in front of the closet door.

Measure the approximate width and length of each piece of furniture you'd like in your room and on the colored poster paper draw a series of small, different shapes using the same 1-inch to 1-foot scale. To the nonartists among us: Remember that the desk or table doesn't actually have to look like a tiny desk or table but should be a round or perhaps a rectangular shape (drawn to approximate scale) that represents the object. You don't have to be exact in these measurements, but use common sense. If the poster-paper shape of the couch is not larger than the desk, something's wrong.

On your plan, make sure you leave room for practical traffic patterns: People need easy access to couches, chairs, and dining areas.

After you've drawn your basic floor plan, it's easier to experiment with arrangements by pushing around paper patterns instead of the actual furniture. Play with balance (do I really want the couch and the fireplace on the same wall?) and function (will guests be able to converse easily?) until you get a sense that—*Yes,* this is comfortable! This will really work.

And that's the formula: FSC.

Function, Style and Comfort are the key to the good and beautiful life at home.

scale: 3/16 inch = 1 foot

Step 1: Measure room and indicate windows and doors.

Step 2: Measure, draw, and cut out furniture.

Step 3: Experiment, then place cutouts. Allow for traffic patterns.

LEGEND

X   Window

Y   Fireplace

Z   Archway

⊠   Outlet

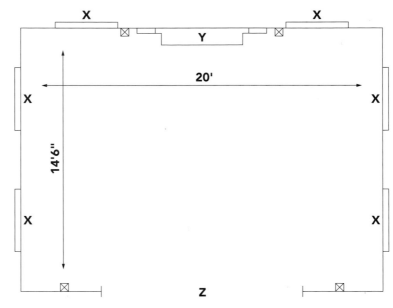

FLOOR PLAN OF EMPTY ROOM

LEGEND

A   rug, 9 x 12 feet

B   sofa, 7 x 3 feet

C   sofa table, 5 x 2 feet

D   basket with dried flowers

E   chair, 18 x 24 inches

F   club chair, 33 x 30 inches

G   end table, 18 x 18 inches

H   tea cart, 24 x 36 inches

I   clock

J   wing chair, 34 x 30 inches

K   table, 12 x 18 inches

L   coffee table, 24 x 66 inches

⊕   lighting

✳ ❀   plants

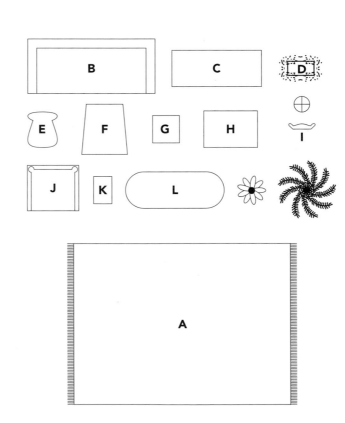

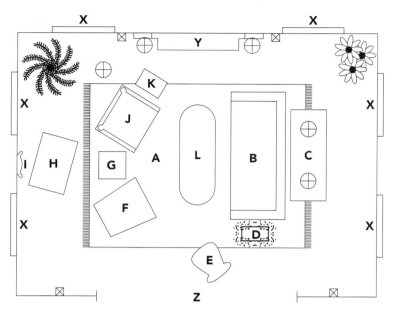

FLOOR PLAN OF FILLED ROOM

*T*he *finished living room: The plump sofa and wing and club chairs are icons of comfort. Many handy surfaces attend the furniture. Behind the sofa is a large serving table; in front is an antique iron and glass coffee table. Each chair is flanked by a convenient table, and an antique wicker cart serves as a bar. The eye is immediately drawn to a golden silk, heavily fringed scarf throw over a chair arm—a symbol of luxurious warmth.* Design by Teri Seidman Interiors; photography by Bates Photography.

B*ook-lined walls, plump cushions, a soothing view, and a dollop of sherry warm the heart.*

Design by Alvin Schneider Design, Inc.; photography by Derrick-Love.

II WHAT'S YOUR DESIGN UMBRELLA?

....

Let's talk pure style for a moment.

You need to choose a design umbrella—a look that will remain reasonably constant throughout your home. We know that a room decorated half in Early Americana and half in Art Deco will project neither character nor radiance. Although you can stray a bit from the overall look and add special effects from other decorating styles, in your own mind you must firmly see the embracing, general cover of one particular design umbrella. Then, on a glorious shopping spree, you'll have the willpower to turn down the almost-irresistible grandfather clock for your southwestern-flavored living room.

But what if you're not sure which look is the look of your dreams?

Take this quiz to find out.

Approach it with a lightness of spirit. Your answers won't change the world. What they will do, upon analysis of your preferences and personality, is give you an insight into your personal tastes and help you decorate a home so pretty, it *looks* just right!

Only after you choose your design umbrella to determine overall style can you then concentrate on comfort—on making your home *feel* just right.

1. YOU HAVE A FREE DAY—WHAT WOULD YOU MOST LIKE TO DO?
a. Go see the exhibit of French tapestries at the Cloisters museum
b. Go see the exhibit of Frederic Remington sculptures at the Museum of American Art
c. Browse in bookstores for architectural prints
d. Laze around in an Adirondack hunting lodge
e. Work in the garden

2. ABOUT YOUR CLOTHES—YOU *REALLY* LOVE YOUR:
a. silk chemises
b. L.L. Bean jeans
c. Reeboks
d. Ralph Lauren cowboy shirt
e. feet pajamas

3. AFTER AN HOUR AT THE BORING COCKTAIL PARTY, YOU LONG FOR YOUR:

a. French chaise

b. cushioned Windsor chair

c. Eames chair

d. twig easy chair

e. wicker rocker

4. YOUR IDEA OF COMFORT FOOD IS:

a. either porridge or crêpes with fresh raspberries and crème fraîche

b. steak

c. tofu, radicchio salad, frozen yogurt

d. chiles rellenos

e. pancakes

5. THE FABRIC THAT MAKES YOU SIGH WITH HAPPINESS IS:

a. damask

b. denim

c. Ultrasuede

d. Mexican cotton

e. gingham

6. YOUR DREAM VACATION? YOU'LL BE STAYING AT:

a. a Victorian-English bed and breakfast

b. the inn where George Washington slept

c. the Golden Door spa

d. an Adirondack lodge

e. your cousin's farmhouse

7. YOUR IDEA OF SWELL TRANSPORTATION IS A:

a. Rolls-Royce

b. fine-spirited horse

c. Japanese bullet train

d. Jeep or a beach buggy

e. old-fashioned sleigh

8. IF YOU COULD DANCE THE NIGHT AWAY, YOU'D:

a. waltz

b. lindy

c. vogue

d. do a Texas two-step

e. square-dance

9. WHAT DRIVES YOU NUTS?
a. not knowing your roots
b. snide anti-Americanism
c. tassels
d. landscapes without character
e. cities

10. THE ART YOU LOVE IS:
a. ancestor portraits
b. brass eagle sculptures and Audubon prints
d. utterly linear or abstract work
e. Mexican pottery or driftwood sculpture
f. patchwork quilts, rooster weather vanes, painted wooden figures

11. YOU LIKE TO BE THOUGHT OF AS:
a. traditionalist
b. patriotic
c. avant-garde
d. adventurer in ethnic food and style
e. natural

12. KEEP YOUR DACHSHUND AND GIVE ME:
a. an English springer spaniel
b. a collie
c. a greyhound
d. a pet iguana
e. a calico cat

13. IF YOU WERE GETTING MARRIED, YOU'D HOPE SOMEONE WOULD BUY YOU:
a. a crystal chandelier
b. antique pewter candlesticks
c. a computer
d. an authentic Navajo rug
e. a handstitched sampler

14. IF YOU WERE REDECORATING YOUR BATHROOM, A GREAT TOUCH WOULD BE:
a. an ornate silver vanity set
b. a miniature Queen Anne wing chair for towel storage
c. a stereo and tape deck
d. the sun-bleached horns of a desert creature as wall art
e. a rag rug on a heated floor

15. IF YOU WERE GIVING A DINNER PARTY FOR IMPORTANT CLIENTS, WHAT WOULD YOU USE FOR FLOWERS ON THE TABLE?

a. English porcelain flowers as a centerpiece

b. wild sage grasses artistically strewn on each napkin

c. one dramatic white orchid on a Lucite stand

d. a gorgeous cactus plant on a hand-painted plate

e. a basket of wild field flowers

16. WHAT MAKES YOU FEEL MOST COMFORTABLE?

a. *lushness*—pillows, pillows, more pillows on a richly tapestried sofa

b. *polished patinas*—a Philadelphia highboy, a grandfather clock and a brass spittoon

c. *sleekness*—glass, steel, leather, a monochromatic ambience

d. *regional charm*—Santa Fe camp, New England saltbox, Adirondack cabin

e. *warmth*—hammocks, botanical prints, wood-burning kitchen stove

17. THE ROOM IN YOUR HOME THAT SOMEHOW NEVER FELT JUST RIGHT— AND THE BEST REASON WHY—IS:

a. my bedroom because it's not a place where I feel deliciously, feet-up pampered. I want it to be more luxurious, more—*plump!*

b. my dining room because it seems to be lacking a sense of *history*

c. my home office because it seems so cluttered with *stuff,* and yet it's non-functional. I don't feel I want to spend a lot of time in this room—and yet I have to. Bottom line? It doesn't work like a dream.

d. none of the rooms feel, well, *appropriate*—they just don't seem to complement the character of the surrounding landscape.

e. my kitchen because it simply doesn't evoke the sense of warmth, coziness, or camaraderie I so admire

18. YOU'D NEVER GET UP IN THE MORNING IF YOU COULD SLEEP ON A:

a. four-poster bed under a gathered-silk canopy

b. hand-hewn wooden Shaker bed

c. durable leather office couch

d. white wrought-iron bed with a fishnet canopy

e. stenciled wooden bed warmed by a patchwork quilt

19. RIGHT NOW, AS YOU DO THIS QUIZ, THE ENTRYWAY TO YOUR HOME IS:

a. lavishly, lushly silver and velvety inviting

b. decorated with Currier and Ives prints, an Early American wall mural, or lace—somewhere!

c. chic and simple, pure and bare, probably black and white

d. inviting with its regional charisma

e. made charming by a primitive painting or other "country" art

20. Comfort seems to come with:

a. skirted tables, fringed hassocks, antique brocades, timeworn patinas, a green velvet Baroque settee

b. historical scenes, William and Mary chairs, piecrust tea tables, Paul Revere silver

c. monochromatic color, geometrics, glass and steel, architectural columns

d. indigenous color, rustic twig furniture or southwestern art, or the grace of an ocean cottage

e. acres and acres of organdy, wicker porch furniture, stenciled walls, cows, cows, and more cows.

Analysis

Did You Choose Mostly A's?

Your design umbrella is Fine Traditional. You are drawn to the sensuality of plushness and color—usually with classic European opulence. You can read the poetry in lavishly trimmed fabric drapes, in a magnificent canopied bed, even in the mystery of traditional Oriental decor. You are drawn to needlepoint-covered stools, tassels, portraits of ancestors—*anyone's* ancestors. Pretty things all around—collections, ribbons, and floral hatboxes make you feel comfortable, safe, and pleasured. You pay attention to the feel of your sheets, and you love to stretch out on furniture, like a cat. You crave luxury and elegance, and while your earthy, pleasure-loving self appreciates practicality, you basically want to decorate with lush, sink-in comfort in mind.

Did You Choose Mostly B's?

Your design umbrella is Classic Americana. Although you're not married *only* to things American, you feel drawn to the classically dark wood-warmed furniture made comfortable with printed toiles or brocade upholstery that looks as if it were designed by Early American craftspeople. You admire symbols that evoke this country's heritage—framed copies of historical documents, high-backed chairs, wood paneling on walls, tea tables heavy with silver or pewter. Comfort, for you, comes with pedigree and the richness of antiques or excellent reproductions of antiques. You couldn't live without a grandfather clock or a wing chair.

Did You Choose Mostly C's?

Your design umbrella is Sleek Contemporary. For you, the most important aspect of comfort is contained in high-tech quality, both practically and visually. Chances are you work in your home either full- or part-time; perhaps you are a master at entertaining, a very creative homemaker. In order for you to feel pleasure in your home, it must run efficiently—that energizes you. If you have to *think* about where to put the keys, the snow boots, the groceries, or the clothes you've just taken off, you'll always have a vague sense of discomfort. For you, the classics of contemporary appeal most broadly—the bentwood, Vilpuri, Barcelona, or Wassily chairs which are built on bold, simple lines. You enjoy the comfort of superb storage—no clutter, knickknacks, or straw baskets dilute the drama of simplicity. The look is linear—smooth and unbroken.

DID YOU CHOOSE MOSTLY D'S?

Your design umbrella is Regional Flair. You love a look that complements the surrounding environment—whether it's the rustic logs, bricks, and stones that are used in creative Adirondack style (bear rugs, wildlife paintings, pine ceiling beams) or desert-inspired terra-cotta with accents of sand, stone, and wood. It could be the sun-bleached whites and wicker of a beach house, or the colorful Native-American craft colors of a Santa Fe lodge. You admire a look that tells you where you are, or where you'd most like to be.

Interestingly enough, many of us seem to be heading into the North Woods these days, with the influences of designers like Ralph Lauren and television shows like *Twin Peaks* and *Northern Exposure.* Decors inspired by this school of interior design are chic wilderness outposts that are worlds away from fancy European formalism.

For you, comfort is in the eclectic—the odd funky rusticity you discover in a treasure from travel or even the local flea market. Comfort also lies in the unexpected—in surprises and in charisma. *Your* home must have personality. You find comfort in the simple life.

DID YOU CHOOSE MOSTLY E'S?

Your design umbrella is Tranquil Country. You appreciate the safe, snug, and warm. Whether you see your home as formal, English garden kind of country or tea cozy kind of country, a back-to-basics attitude looms large. If you can have curl-up corners and relaxing nooks and niches in your rooms, you're a happy camper. You prefer informal rather than formal dining and handcrafted rather than machine made. Your joys are collections of animals, quilts, plants, folk art or anything weatherworn.

You admire champagne—but you also love a steaming cup of hot chocolate. You'd choose Grandma's hand-embroidered tea towels over someone else's Mondrian-inspired facecloth; a pillow-backed deacon's bench in your brass-potted kitchen over a buttery-leather lounger in someone else's living room; a warm, spice-smelling, Welsh-cupboarded dining room over the most elegant restaurant.

Voluptuous comfort: A sensual bedroom is our safe place. . . . Design by Stephen Mallory; photography by Kari Haavisto.

III VOLUPTUOUS COMFORT

....

The lust for comfort,
that stealthy thing that enters
the house a guest, and then
becomes a host, and then, a master.
—KAHLIL GIBRAN

The poet Gibran chose his words carefully. The *lust* for comfort does seem to take over. The sensual appeal of deep plush pillows and body-tranquillizing furniture is absolutely riveting.

Voluptuaries who worship at the altar of the senses decorate their homes to gratify those senses. Their brand of comfort is gentle. It can also be stylish, usable, and personal. Most of all, it must feel good.

The Voluptuously Comfortable Bedroom

Although other rooms in your home may be decorated with voluptuous comfort in mind, surely the room which most epitomizes sensual pleasure is the bedroom. In the midst of a busy, tiring day, who among us has not lusted for a deliciously calming bed or an enveloping chaise?

Of all the rooms in our public and private lives, the bedroom is also the most intimate. Even if we occasionally invite others into the bedroom, it still remains a personal sanctuary where one's true essence is allowed to breathe free. It is in the bedroom where we strip off veneers and, sighing with relief, stretch out like cats.

The bedroom is our safe place.

It is also the place where we play, dream, recharge, and prepare for the next day.

Imagine an uncomfortable bedroom filled with sharp edges, beautiful but untouchable fabrics, and no table at which to sip a cup of tea or write a letter to a lover. The thought is enough to make a voluptuary wince.

Function

Remember the FSC formula: *Function first, then Style, then Comfort.*

Consider function by deciding what you want your bedroom to do—besides provide a place to sleep. Answer the questions in the Comfort Zone checklist to help you determine all the functions of your bedroom.

Style

Using the FSC formula, you've determined the function of your bedroom by completing the Comfort Zone checklist.

Now, consider the style in which you'll decorate. The quiz in chapter

COMFORT ZONE CHECKLIST: THE BEDROOM

THE BED

Who sleeps in your bed—just you, or you and your partner?

If you sleep with another, do you prefer fitting like spoons in a double or queen-sized bed—or do you need your space in a king-sized bed?

Besides sleeping on your bed, do you use it to:

eat

make love

work or pay bills

talk on the telephone

read

play games, sew, do exercises

watch TV or listen to music

perform beauty rituals (nails, makeup, etc.)?

ELECTRONIC COMFORT

Decide where it's most comfortable for you to keep controls and appliances—near your bed, easy chair, or desk? Check to see that there are enough socket outlets for your needs.

Electronics might include:

TV, radio and stereo

computer

coffee or tea maker

telephone/answering machine

alarm clock

lamps

burglar alarms

intercoms

STORAGE

Where do you put your clothes as soon as you take them off?

Do you need extra or built-in storage—perhaps a freestanding armoire?

Do you need improved bedside storage?

SOUND AND LIGHT

Do you prefer waking to darkness or sunlight?

Will you need an isolated reading light over your bed (to avoid bothering your partner), mood lights, or high-intensity work lights?

Do you find comfort in quiet? Will you need to soundproof with carpet, throw rugs, and heavy curtains?

SEATING

For your own or your partner's comfort, which do you prefer—a chaise, club chair, rocker? Do you have room for more than one comfort chair?

Will you dine in your bedroom? How about others? For the comfort of those who may share conversation, food, or entertainment in your bedroom, what kind of seating or tables will you need?

PSYCHIC COMFORT

Do you need privacy when you dress?

Do certain colors unruffle your feathers?

Do you feel happiest when surrounded by things you love—collections, old photographs, botanical prints?

Are you especially sensitive to touch? Have you investigated fabrics (kid, suede, velvets) that feel great and can be treated for longer wear?

Are you particularly sensitive to smell? Do you need to think about extra (or more efficient) laundry or shoe storage to avoid unpleasant odors?

GUESTS

Do guests also feel voluptuous comfort in the place you've provided? Do they have to ask for items they need—or have you thoughtfully anticipated those needs?

EXERCISE

If you have set aside an area in or near your bedroom for your workouts, is it as comfortable as a professional health club?

II has given you some ideas, your own research has guided you in certain directions, and at this point perhaps you'll want to draw a design umbrella to help yourself pinpoint the details.

COMFORT

The last step of the FSC process is to consider Comfort. Now, you can begin to decorate your bedroom for comfort.

THE BED

Every bedroom needs a starting point, a center of attraction, and since each of us sleeps away a third of our lives—about 220,000 hours—it makes sense that the bed takes center stage. Even if your bedroom is a multipurpose room with many secondary functions that are almost as important as sleeping, that bed is still queen of the roost. Your friends may think of your bed as a living room on springs, your mate may think of it as a place of sleep and love, but for a sensualist like you, the bed's the place where your body and soul find warmth, support, and safety. Because decorating is about relationships, the bed is also the place from which every other piece of furniture in the room will take its cue.

By this time, depending on the way you like to sleep (by yourself or with a partner) and depending on the amount of room you have available, you know whether you want a single, double, queen-sized, or king-sized bed.

Voluptuous beds come in three personal styles: Which one fits under your design umbrella?

THE SWEEPING SHELTER

This is the totally enclosed bed that feels like a little womb. It is a throwback to medieval days when castle occupants engulfed themselves in lush, hanging fabrics to keep out castle drafts. It's a bed for Sleeping Beauty, a hideout, a refuge. It's usually a canopied four-poster with an extravagant profusion of material draped on top and around the sides of the superstructure.

THE SEMISHELTER

Some feel comfortable with just a suggestion of enclosure, and the semishelter comes in many wood or metal variations of the four-poster, among them:
- full-canopied four-poster with no attached side fabric
- ornately carved four-poster without a canopy
- simple, linear outline of a four-poster—perhaps with an unconstructed piece of fabric draped over the top
- half or quarter canopy

A *sweeping shelter: a totally enclosed sanctuary . . .*

Design by Patricia Sayers for Mansions & Millionaires; photography by Oleg March.

The *semisheltered bed: With only a suggestion of a canopy, the bed still feels protective. Its black, linear architecture echoes the calligraphy of the shielding screen.*

Design by Anthony Antine; photography by Bill Rothschild.

The unfenced shelter: an open, expansive bed, peaceful and welcoming. The sleek, contemporary built-ins are gentled by the patterned rug.

Design by Richard Mervis Design, Inc.; photography by Bill Rothschild.

THE UNFENCED SHELTER

This is an open, expansive bed with or without a head or footboard. It comes in many style variations, including the famous sleigh bed, and its interest often derives from carved, hand-painted, or upholstered head and footboards. I like to have such headboards upholstered in a quilted version of the fabric I've chosen for the windows. The unfenced shelter's comfort relies on its sense of disclosure, its unobstructed welcome. It may be piled high with fat, lavish pillows or it may be simple and starkly adorned, but it's always invitingly exposed and peaceful.

Shop around before you settle on a bed style. Try out your friends' beds and feel free to test department store models. You may discover that a sweeping shelter feels suspiciously like prison instead of the womb or that an unfenced shelter makes you feel uncomfortably vulnerable.

Also remember that your bed style will be key to the rest of the room style. A sweeping-shelter canopy bed with richly gathered, lavishly trimmed fabric would best be served by the carved moldings, elaborate silver, tasseled accessories, skirted tables, and complementary (not necessarily identical) window fabric of a Fine Traditional bedroom. Conversely, a starkly contemporary chrome four-poster would most logically be served by sleek Italian lamps, abstract art, and classic contemporary furniture.

Although provocative surprises add drama, good interior design requires control; accessories should never be thrown in willy-nilly, but with regard to the design umbrella.

BEDDING

THE MATTRESS

Once your bed style has been determined, your personal comfort next rests on what's *on* the bed. Will you feel best on:

- a waterbed?
- a board-supported, extra-firm innerspring mattress?
- a body-sculpting soft mattress?
- a foam mattress?
- a futon (usually made of layers of cotton, wool, foam, and horsehair)?

It is safe to say that the more you pay, the better the quality. Don't stint on a mattress or box spring because they will be unseen. Your entire sense of well-being depends on where you slept the night before.

TIPS ON BUYING A MATTRESS

Look for more than 300 coils in a full-size innerspring, more than 375 in a queen size and more than 450 in a king size.

The mattress covering should be of natural fibers so the mattress can breathe.

Consider mattress thickness. Mattresses have always ranged from ascetic to pampering. The classic sack of straw that for centuries prevailed as a mattress in Europe gave way to the mattresses of medieval France, which were so plump in the households of the nobles that servants were assigned to poke the bedding to make sure no assassins lurked inside.

In more recent decades, everyone's back woes have led to the rise of the extra-firm mattress, and manufacturers, sensing a trend to comfort decorating, are once again offering thick, thick, thick mattresses. In extreme cases a lush 16-inch thickness now replaces the standard 7-inch-thick mattresses. Also available are what the manufacturers call "pillow tops"—quilted pads placed over and under a mattress; no princess will ever feel a pea.

THE BEDCLOTHING

The right sheet and the perfect pillowcase are always of prime importance to a dreamy sleep.

Synthetics: There are distinct advantages to bedclothing made of synthetic fibers: The wonderful new blends are enormously appealing to the allergic among us and also to the wary consumer, mindful of easy-care, well-priced products. Today, synthetic sheets and cases come in attractive prints and vibrant, coordinated solids.

Naturals: To the purist, sheets and pillowcases of natural fibers boast thermal qualities for warmth in winter and coolness in summer. Your choices:

All cotton—domestic white percale with a typical weave of 200 threads per square inch is the classic. Cotton comes in different qualities, so experiment to find the most comfortable for you.

Natural linen—expensive but divinely comfortable, linen sheets can be woven as tightly as 1,500 threads per square inch. They outlast all others, and repeated washings actually strengthen the fabric. The downside to linen is that it *must* be ironed—even the cotton-linen blends.

Silk—also a natural fiber, is elegant and luxurious but considerably less practical than other naturals because it snags and runs. Talk about the height of sybaritic pleasure, though, and you're talking silk sheets.

Cotton flannel—provides extra warmth and softness.

Heirloom bedding—expensive but big in the emotional comfort department are heirloom sheets—always in natural fibers. Found in specialty shops, these have been preserved from someone else's past, and the lace and crochet trousseaux of long-ago brides seem to have their own memories. It's easy to understand how the everyday use of antique bed-clothing can have a great calming effect.

TIP: Some specialty bedding stores will trim sheets and cases to match an unusual fabric or wallpaper, and this elegant touch is wonderful for pulling a room together.

BED COVERINGS

- Quilts—meant to warm and comfort without feeling like a ton of bricks. It's no accident that quilts are often called "comforters." The lightest, warmest, most delicious quilts are constructed in three parts—a top, a lining, and a backing filled with pure down (eider duck, white goose, and regular duck down—in order from most to least expensive). Quilts filled with feather and down combinations are the next best (the more down, the better the quilt). Quilts with wool fillings are at the bottom of the list. Synthetically filled quilts are available for people allergic to feathers; today they can be stylish and well priced. Also available are silk- or cotton-filled quilts.
- Blankets—the most comfortable are cashmere, merino wool, long-pile mohair, and pure cotton. Blankets of synthetic fabric are inexpensive and widely available.
- Throws—the voluptuously comfortable bedroom usually sports one

made of pure mohair or cashmere, thrown casually on the bed or on the back of a comfortable chair—just right for snuggling.

PILLOW TALK

Pillows to sleep on . . .

Duck or goose down filled—the best choice for the nonallergic. Down and feather combinations are also available, and all can be found in firm, medium, or soft densities.

Polyester—nonallergenic and germ repellent and available in different densities, but they shouldn't even be mentioned in a book on comfort decorating except to note that they're available if needed.

Neck pillows shaped like a roll, or boudoir or baby-sized pillows also add immeasurably to a perfect night's sleep.

Never buy a pillow without testing it. Fluff it with your hands to check its density; then, keeping its sanitary cover on, actually lay your head on it to see if you feel like taking it home.

Pillows to show off . . .

Throw pillows meant for display on your bed are not usually meant for sleeping; still, natural-fabric fillings even *look* more comfortable than synthetic. They can be squashed and pushed into appealing, "mushy" shapes.

Most pillows, irrespective of bedspread or quilt color, look wonderful in pure white or embroidered linen. Others look gorgeous in colorful solids, checks or florals that harmonize with other fabrics in the room. Some pillows are wreathed, some scalloped, some embroidered and tasseled; other show-off pillows are lavished with lace. Many are antique. All should whisper—*comfortable.*

ARE BEDSPREADS STILL ALLOWED?

In the old days, everyone had one. Sometimes they were fitted and sometimes they were loose throws, but each bed had a bedspread to cover the blanket and sheets and provide a finishing touch. Today, we use our beds for more than sleeping, and bedspreads seem to have lost much of their appeal. We are living in the era of the artfully unmade bed. What is called the "open bed" has come into nineties favor—the comfortably rumpled, plushly quilted, splendidly pillow-layered open bed. One rises in the morning, straightens one's duvet (a down- or feather-filled comforter), and the bed is "made."

For those in whom old habits die hard, bedspreads are still a possibil-

A cozy love seat on which to dream, read, or sip a glass of wine makes the room more than a place to sleep.

Linens by Louis Nicole for Martex; photography by Feliciano.

ity. Simple light basket or waffle weaves, crocheted or knitted fabrics, and other textures are options, as are more formal, tapestrylike materials.

For the ultimate in bedspread comfort, consider the nubby, nostalgic chenille spread. It is the textile equivalent of chocolate grahams and milk, redolent with memories. The chenille spread will satisfy anyone's longing for the quintessentially comfortable childhood home.

INTIMATE TURFS

The furniture in a comfortable bedroom should reflect our heart's pleasures. It creates a sense of the private turf where we lounge, eat, play games, dream, dress, store our belongings, and reconstitute our images.

THE SECRETS OF THE NIGHT TABLE

In the drawers of night tables and on their surfaces lie maps to our most private selves. What do we really read when we are alone and safe from judgmental eyes? What are those scraps of paper with the mysterious telephone numbers and snippets of names? Why do we feel compelled to keep the multiple pairs of eyeglasses whose prescriptions have grown stronger through the years?

Here are the contraceptives for lovemaking, the address books, the pills, the tissues, the glass for the 3 A.M. drink of water, the paper pads and pencils, all the *stuff* that we've shoved away—just to get it away. The night

A *small bureau becomes a commodious night table to hide secrets and display treasures. A bench becomes a go-anywhere table.*

Courtesy of Richard E. Thibaut, Inc.

table keeps its secrets comfortably unless it is too small or too decorative to be of real use. Look for a night table with:

- generous surface space for a lamp, telephone, answering machine and a calming cup of tea; the best night tables have drawers or doored spaces to hold the remote controls to your stereo, television, lighting, locking-up and alarm setting for the entire house.
- ample, accessible drawers; for example, if you love the look of a covered, skirted table (try a drapery fabric topped with an antique-lace throw) use one on one side of your bed, but use a night table with a reachable drawer on the other side.

Many of us have pressed drawerless, more eclectic choices into service as night tables. Antique garden stools, Victorian washstands, painted French children's chairs, small desks, and English library steps are all charming possibilities. Square nightstands can be transformed into skirted tables by topping them with plywood circles and covering them with floor-length skirts. But we still need places to put our hair clips, face creams, and pencil stubs.

Solutions

On top of the night table or dresser try a collection of small boxes in wicker, wood, papier-mâché, or painted enamel, some with lids closed, others left open.

Small antique dentist's cabinets or miniature chests of drawers look wonderful on the eclectic night table. Twig baskets make interesting holders.

Trays provide a "pulled together" look for pretty covered bowls hiding night-table secrets.

A stack of delicate floral hatboxes or an old trunk can be a creative night table and just the thing to hold your reading or needlepoint as well as show off the silver-topped crystal jars, photographs, and collection of rare tortoiseshell combs.

THE GO-ANYWHERE TABLE

For some, the most intimately comfortable turf is plunk in the middle of the bed; comfort for these people is about working or eating on a pretty bed tray. Make it sturdy but light; there's nothing comfortable about twenty pounds of bed tray resting on your abdomen.

For most of us, though, bedroom ease depends on having a place to live that is separate from the bed. The best way to create such a private corner is with a small go-anywhere table—perhaps in Victorian bamboo, painted wood, or functional glass. The table, flanked by two small but comfortable chairs, is called "go anywhere" because, usually placed in a snug

*Sybaritic spots: His
and her dressing rooms,
lavishly tented, are
private, safe harbors.*

Design by Teri Seidman Interiors
at Mansions & Millionaires;
photography by Oleg March.

nook or in front of a window, it's not so heavy that it can't be moved to serve many needs, a game of backgammon, the reading of the Sunday newspaper, or consuming the pizza delivery.

SYBARITIC SPOT

Vanities or dressing tables are back, and there's nothing as personally satisfying as a well-lit, beautifully mirrored area to indulge in personal inspection and reconstruction. It is a sanctuary as well as an image work-place and one should feel comfortable spending a long, sybaritic half hour here.

Vanities can be sleek Italian, avant-garde geometric, or the frilly, kidney-shaped versions you remember from your girlhood. Choose one that will carry out the point of view of the rest of the room.

The placement of the vanity is what will determine your level of comfort. For many, including me, the best place to apply makeup is in daylight, so my dressing table is near a window. Other women only feel comfortable making up near a sink: Their vanities must be placed near the bathroom. It looks expensive and difficult but in actuality it's reasonably inexpensive and simple to run the bathroom plumbing into your bedroom to position a pretty extra sink near your vanity.

Don't think in decorating clichés when it comes to dressing tables: Any charming table with a freestanding mirror (turn-of-the-century, three-way "triptych" mirrors are gorgeous and ubiquitous in antique stores) can serve as a vanity. I've used Parsons tables and a half-round pine table with a garden chair to nice advantage. Where space was sparse, I've put a fine Limoges porcelain tray for cosmetics on a night table and pressed it into doing double duty as a vanity.

A word about vanity chairs: Choose the prettiest, most unique chair you can find—it can be frilly, handsome, carved, tailored, or upholstered, no matter the style of the vanity it serves. Because they are "one-of-a-kind," these chairs can be a touch of contrast.

Search for this special chair in antique stores, auction houses, or "boutique" furniture stores. Because you're not looking for a set, the wonderful, single chair should not be difficult to find. Remember that, because it's your special chair, it should fit you perfectly. Its height, width, and plushness should be just right for you.

BIG EASY NICHE

The Victorians called it a "fainting chair," in deference to the allegedly delicate nature of Victorian women.

I call it the "Big Easy"—the engulfing, soothing, stretch-out-into chaise longue (long chair), often mistakenly referred to as a chaise *lounge*. It is the essence of comfort furniture, and if it were up to me, I'd put a chaise in every room of the house, including the bathroom and kitchen. A chaise is the perfect safe place.

Originally, chaises were only boudoir chairs and always sumptuously upholstered and cushioned for comfort. They were primarily found in women's private sanctuaries and were used for reflection, seduction, writing, and refreshment of the soul and body—along with fainting. Today, recognizing that men have similar comfort needs, chaises also come in sleek, architect's sculptural shapes in leather, suede, and other bold fabrics and colors.

A bedroom chaise takes the same accessories you'd use on a bed—a tray for a meal, an adjacent short-legged table for a writing or reading surface, a marvelous mohair throw for chill moments. European-size, neckroll, and boudoir pillows in appropriate fabrics make a chaise even more comfortable.

THE COMFORT CORNER

Here's a tip: *Corners* are nurturing, safe places. A country or formal French armoire (depending on your design umbrella), a chintz or velvet love seat with an ottoman, and a tiny round table all tucked neatly into a corner bring living room comfort into the privacy of the bedroom.

DRESSING UP

The most private turf of all is the place where you dress. Some people can pull on clothing any old place in the house, but some of us feel more comfortable in a secluded corner where we can completely take stock of ourselves, try on, take off, and in general feel happily unobserved even by loving eyes. Of course, an irresistible luxury is a traditional dressing room attached to the bedroom and set up with convenient storage space, chairs on which to sit as we draw on stockings, and mirrors, mirrors, mirrors.

But dressing rooms don't have to be attached to bedrooms. Any tiny, unused room will do, and here storage space can be more visible than it would be in the middle of your bedroom—utilizing, for example, manufacturers' dress racks for clothes and open wire-rack shelving for underwear. If such a tiny, unused room does not exist, consider carving out a small private corner in the bedroom by bumping out an unused closet or bathroom or by simply screening off a few feet of space.

Comfortable dressing requires easy access: I once had a client who, in the interest of space-saving, put her bureau in her closet behind a row of hanging clothes, thereby making sure she had to *work* to open those bureau drawers. We took the bureau from the closet, carved out a 6-foot square area in her bedroom, lined one wall with floor-to-ceiling storage shelves, put a freestanding, full-length, nineteenth-century tulipwood cheval mirror against the other wall, painted the ceiling with a trompe l'oeil sky to give the illusion of space (and also to give purposeful boundaries to this special corner) and *voilà!*—she suddenly had the most charming dressing room in the world!

KILLER CLUTTER

There's no way to feel comfort in chaos. Keeping things neat makes rooms seem larger and more appealing. The hard news is that most of our personal possesions, not to mention our clothes, live in the bedroom. In a perfect world, there'd be a place for everything and everything in its place behind a giant wall of unobtrusive doors—but since the world is not perfect, let us consider some of the biggest storage solutions, one by one.

STORAGE UNITS

BUILT-INS

Modular units offer an endless number of arrangements and storage opportunities and since they are sold separately, you can tailor them to your needs.

Extending a unit all the way along a wall to the door makes a room seem larger.

For smaller rooms, "disappearing" modular units—painted, papered, or covered to match the rest of the walls—appear to increase wall space because they don't stand out.

Fitted units that feature shallow drawers are more efficient than those with deep drawers; see-through acrylic or wire drawers allow you to keep track of socks and shirts.

Inexpensive units can be customized by changing handles or by painting or replacing doors with mirrored versions that seem to expand space and light.

Wardrobes and a run of high cupboards can be built all around a window, in essence framing the window. A shelf right under the windowsill can make a compact, useful desk or makeup table. If you choose the latter, pretty and unusual boxes can hold daylight makeup that is quite different from the makeup you store in the bathroom.

The addition of a window seat can do more for a bedroom than just add a romantic nook. Again, frame the seat with storage shelves from floor to ceiling (and under the seat).

Side cabinets with smoky-glass fronts will look airy and can also conceal linens or laundry.

ARMOIRES, HIGHBOYS, LOWBOYS, AND OTHER STORAGE GEMS

The Armoire has been around at least since the Renaissance. The word derives from *armarium,* Latin for cupboard, which in turn comes from *arma*—meaning weapons. Armoires are carefully constructed, freestanding containers enclosed by doors for men's and women's clothes. An armoire is a piece of architecture, a building in miniature with organized interior space and a beautiful outer shell. It's a powerful piece of bedroom furniture because its height is commanding and it can accommodate so much. Of course, armoires can be converted for china storage or entertainment centers, but first and foremost, they can be personally fitted for storing clothing on shelves, in drawers, and hanging from rods.

The dressing chest, commonly called a "dresser," is a shorter chest with drawers to contain clothes and other belongings; its lower height almost always invites a beautiful wall mirror to crest it.

The highboy is a tall chest of drawers with a flat or elaborately carved top and varied drawer arrangements, depending on its style. Another form of highboy is called a "chest on chest," which, although one piece of furniture, often has a narrower set of drawers perched on a wider set, giving the illusion of two separate chests on top of each other.

The lowboy is a much smaller chest, often just a small table with one, two, or three drawers; it is frequently used as a dressing table.

A chest is a large box with a hinged lid, often used to store extra linens and blankets at the foot of a bed

A commode is a small, more delicate chest of drawers, frequently used as a night table.

PLACEMENT: WHERE DO WE PUT THESE GEMS?

Place a tall, narrow piece of furniture (like an armoire) at one end of a long wall, but balance it with height on the other end: Try a wonderful tree, artwork, or wall sconces over a small table for pretty balance.

The best place for an armoire that houses a TV is on a wall facing the bed or chair where you settle at night. If this is not possible, the piece can be fitted with a pull-out, swiveling lazy Susan shelf. View-obstructing armoire doors can also be redone so they retract into the piece.

A long double or triple dresser requires a long wall; make sure a large, wonderful piece of art or a beautiful mirror tops it and use the surface of the dresser to display collections or small artwork.

If wall space is limited, consider a smaller chest for your wall and use another small chest as a night table. They do *not* have to match.

TIPS:

- Drawers should slide smoothly and not wobble or stick. The bottoms of the drawers should have center glides and drawer stops to prevent the drawers from accidentally being pulled all the way out.
- The best wooden drawer joints are not nailed: they are made from interlocking wood.
- Storage furniture should have finishes that are smooth; color should be uniform and grains matched.
- Hardware should be of *great* quality: Even an inexpensive piece looks richly elegant if its hinges and drawer pulls are beautiful and they line up neatly.
- Storage gems come in materials suitable to any design umbrella: These include lacquer, metal, or painted and natural woods like oak, cedar, cherry, maple, or pine.

THAT REAL ESTATE TREASURE: THE CLOSET

Anything can be turned into a clutter trap if it's not well organized, but closets are probably the most ubiquitous offenders. In your home, how many times have clothes fallen into the back of a closet, staying there through the changing seasons? How many standard pole and shelf arrangements in your closets are space-wasting disasters?

Organized clothes closets make people feel good, even competent. Killer closets, crammed full of spring, winter, summer, fall, evening, sports, work, and even dirty clothes demean people.

What to do? I'm a firm believer in skilled help here—in the form of professional closet organizers who come in to evaluate your closet system and then make recommendations about transforming existing closet space into the most efficient storage; they even advise you on what personal items to discard. These professionals can be found in the Yellow Pages under "Organizing" or "Household." *Or,* you can try a really good do-it-yourself closet system that you can buy in many places. Amazing space can be carved out of every available inch of closet—and that includes walls, ceilings, and floors.

I generally advise clients who are decluttering clothes closets to empty out the offending closet on a nearby bed, pitch things they haven't worn (or seen) in three years into cardboard boxes labeled SALVATION ARMY, MOTHER'S ATTIC, CLEANERS, GARBAGE etc., and start from scratch to put everything back with a reasoned system. Incidentally, hall, guest, linen, and utility closets can all be attacked in the same manner.

A REASONED SYSTEM

Decide which clothes you'll hang in closets or other storage units and which you'll fold and put on shelves.

Ask, "How often do I use it?" The most frequently used items, like underwear, should be the most accessible, placed in drawers or wire see-through baskets on shelves. The clothes you wear every day should hang in the front of the closet; evening clothes and "rarely worns" live in the back section or in a closet all by themselves.

Divide most closets into thirds: One third should house a rod for short skirts and blouses with shelf space under and over the rod. One third should be devoted to hanging longer clothes. The last third should be devoted to layers of shelves on which perch wire, wicker, and Lucite see-through baskets for belts, pocketbooks, shirts, underclothes, and anything for which there's no room in a drawer.

Use organizers within the closet: Hooks and pegs or an expanding wooden mug rack can be installed on backs of doors and on walls. Cup hooks screwed into the branches of a freestanding coat tree in a closet corner can hold belts, ties, necklaces, beads, hats, scarves, or bags with chains.

His dream closet: Every shirt and sweater is visible in scooped-out drawers; shoes have drawers of their own; wicker baskets are catchalls; ties are instantly visible on back-of-door rods; double-hung rods hold suits. Every inch is utilized behind bifold doors.

Design by Stephanie Stokes, Inc.; photography by John Hall.

Her not-so-dream closet (above left): Try to find the cream blouse in this mess. Her dream closet (above right): This extra-wide closet is divided into four parts, with organizers and bins making it a pleasure to use.

Courtesy of California Closet Co.

A novel storage concept: Vertical drawers pull out for an instant view of untangled jewelry.

Design by Stephanie Stokes, Inc.; photography by Nancy Hill.

Hangers fitted with pockets hold shoes, bags, gloves, and other small items. What to do with hats? Wig forms nailed along one shelf are perfect! If you stack the hats, line them with tissue paper first.

Use closet alternatives: Freestanding clothes racks (like those found in stores) can be hidden by a decorative screen. If you have an alcove from 5 to 7 feet wide that you use for desk space, install a tension rod above your head for shirts and jackets—and cover it with shutters.

SOFT STORAGE

In any closet-deprived bedroom, and especially in a smaller room where bureaus and chests might seem obtrusive, clothes covered by hanging curtains may be the way to go. One client suspended a piece of molding from pretty chains connected to the ceiling, and soft fabric that matched her wallpaper hung from a rod concealed under the molding. It was an imaginative solution. To shield a utilitarian wall of shelves, another client hung antique-lace curtains that beautifully echoed her lace bedspread.

PRICELESS DECLUTTERERS

Within closets, behind soft storage, and in dressers, declutterers play a strong role:

- Drawer dividers (they work in the kitchen and bathroom also) are key.
- Lucite sweater boxes under a bed are great for off-season scarves, hats, gloves.
- Use double-barred wooden hangers for men's suits and padded or slip-free hangers for dresses and blouses.
- Label everything from pockets on hangers to any box that's not see-through in large, loud letters.
- Hooks and pegs are invaluable for holding last night's pajamas, the tiny bag of scented potpourri, and the belts and handbags that invariably end up on the floor.
- File cabinets are *magic.* Every bedroom needs at least one, and you can buy them in any size (used, very inexpensive models are ubiquitous). Store the cabinet in your closet or in an unused, out-of-the-way corner. If you're really strapped for space, throw a gorgeous covering on the file and use it for an end table, but since you have to lift the covering for access to drawers, this is not the best solution. In the file cabinet, store income tax receipts, photos, stamps, product information and warranty cards, spare batteries, pens and pencils, old report cards, instruction booklets, spare gizmos—*everything* that can be alphabetically labeled. TIP: *Hanging* files are particularly useful as clutter-busters.
- Consider wire shelves for sweaters and shirts worn frequently: The

wire assures that clothes are visible and well ventilated. Add shelf dividers to separate his and her items if you don't have separate closets.

- Stackable baskets are great in closets. On wheels, they're *gorgeously* useful.
- Videotapes are taking over the world. Store them in airtight plastic cases on shelves adjacent to the television set or in drawers.
- Tackle or art supply boxes are used by every savvy declutterer for a multitude of purposes—to hold cosmetics, sewing supplies, children's art supplies, tools, hardware, holiday decorations—use your imagination.
- Magazines create big-time clutter. Keep them in a magazine rack or basket and heartlessly toss all that are more than six months old. TIP: Attach a scissors-on-a-ribbon and a smaller basket to the magazine rack for clipping and storing the articles you can't resist.
- Mail can become a monument to clutter if you don't (a) open it daily, (b) *immediately* discard catalogs and junk mail, and (c) store bills to be paid and letters to be answered in appropriate baskets.

KEEP IT ORGANIZED

I have a client who worked with me for a month on organizing the clutter in her room. We stored things, created easy traffic patterns, and left some lovely empty places in her bedroom. "You changed my life," she told me.

But not for long. She made an off-season trip to her summer home and two antique shops, filled up her car, and within another month, all the lovely empty places were soon crammed up again.

The moral? If your emotional need to be sloppy is greater than the need to have an organized, comfortable home, you'll have to go with it. Personally, I believe that even people who thrive on clutter can keep to organized clutter. It makes living with another person much more comfortable.

PSYCHIC COMFORTS IN THE BEDROOM

For some, a bed with an electronic-control headboard and an electric blanket is the epitome of comfort.

For some, a futon or a goose-down quilt on a chaise is the essence of comfort.

For *all,* the psychic comfort that comes from personalizing the bedroom—both in style and in physical ease—is truly the embodiment of voluptuous comfort.

A *collection should have a unifying link: Here, sterling silver and a lacy dresser scarf pull the collection together.*

Design by Stephanie Stokes, Inc.; photography by Walter Smalling.

Bedroom collections:

These are a few of my favorite things. Intimate collections in a bedroom cushion the hours spent there. Favorite things also lend grand style and personality to a room.

Collections can be displayed on wall, desk, night table, or bureau surfaces. Are you a bookish person? How about a collection of miniature antique sterling silver books. Are you an actress? Try a collection of tragedy and comedy masks on the wall. Were you a happy camper? How about a collage of your trophies, camp shirt, and baseball bat caught in a Lucite display frame? Are you strong on "roots"? How about a collection of your ancestors' photographs or the framed love letters your dad wrote your mom, or a collection of family trees—yours, his, and maybe your favorite author's?

WARM FEET, WARM HEART

Psychic comfort also relies on control of the physical environment in the bedroom. The levels of warmth, light, and sound are subtle inducements to curl up and stay in any room.

It's obvious that cold, drafty, or overheated interiors are antithetical to the whole notion of ease. Not quite so obvious, but crucially important, is the way you feel when you walk around your bedroom. Just as we adjust the room temperature with heat or air-conditioning, we also must adjust floor temperature. Somehow the serenity of a room rises from beneath our feet to flood our whole being. Climbing out of bed, it's difficult to find comfort in the cold touch of a marble, tile, or wood floor as the first welcome to the day. Marble, tile, and wood are very elegant indeed, if they're your style, but a soothing throw rug leading from bed to bathroom seems almost mandatory.

DECORATE THE WARM FLOOR

Personally, my taste runs to solid, neutral shade wall-to-wall carpeting or the layering of several rugs in most bedrooms. Floor coverings not only lend warmth, they also soundproof the room. Psychic comfort is strengthened when we're protected from the jarring noises of the outside world. It's also nice to know that whatever you're doing in your bedroom, you can't be heard in the next room.

Consider an "art on the floor" area rug in a strong, geometric pattern.

Or an original (*never* an imitation) Oriental throw rug.

Think about painted-pattern carpets (in florals for a Tranquil Country look or geometrics for a Sleek Contemporary look) or rug accents on slate, tile, terrazzo, or even brick floors, which incidentally can *look* exceptionally cozy and comfortable.

Cork floors are warm, comfortable, and quiet, and their style can range widely depending on whether they're accented with a rich Persian throw, a pale contemporary dhurrie runner, or a heavy, shaggy Greek flokati rug. Also wonderful is a throw rug in a faux leopard print.

My *very* favorite country and city carpet is made from 100 percent wool "sisal," which is deliciously warm and comfortable and comes in a range of natural colors from off-white to honey. Some prefer a natural sisal carpeting, which is derived from a desert plant; I find it's a scratchy fiber and all wrong for underfoot niceness.

Note: Secure light rugs with mesh backing or hook and loop (Velcro) strips to prevent rugs from "walking." There is nothing comfortable about a dangerous slip on a moving floor.

Final Note: Make your own Comfort Zone checklist for the floor before you decide on the most comfortable flooring. For example:

Will you be lying on the floor, exercising (you'll need mats), sitting, playing, dancing on the floor?

Will you be storing your bicycle or baby carriage in your bedroom and thus have to worry about wheel marks?

How about hair from shedding dogs or cats? What kind of floor covering will best hide it?

Do you want the floor to play up a special architectural detail in your bedroom—a domed ceiling, for example—or intricate ceiling moldings, which may cry out for something *simple* on the floor.

THE SUPER BEDROOM TELEPHONE

Comfort can hide in the telephone. In earlier times, the telephone was just for talking, but today some models even include videophones, which let you see the face behind the voice, and there are a dozen other options for real and psychic ease. Here are some more:

The new cordless telephones allow users to wander as far as a quarter of a mile—wonderful for really big bedrooms.

Cordless telephones can also be programmed. Hammacher Schlemmer, Radio Shack, and other companies offer devices that attach to the base of any cordless phone to turn it into a wireless remote unit that can be programmed to control a television, stereo system, or VCR within the normal range of the telephone.

Volume- and clarity-enhancing units can be purchased for the hard-of-hearing.

Oversized buttons are wonderful for old and young.

The new digital telephone-answering machines allow the user to jump back and forth among messages, deleting and listening selectively.

And if you have no room for a whole home office but still want to take advantage of new technologies, several companies (including Quasar) make home office phones that could fit in a bread box: A compact package includes a cordless telephone, an answering machine, and a combination fax machine/copier.

LET THERE BE LIGHT—OR LET THERE NOT BE LIGHT?

For many, psychic comfort in the bedroom relies on an utter absence of light in the morning. For these people, the *most* efficient solution might be "blackout shades" or perhaps outside shutters that let in air as they block the light.

For others, tranquillity comes from sunlight streaming into the bedroom as they awaken to the morning. They should stick with no window treatments at all, or perhaps the sheerest, softest muslin or unlined cotton curtains.

The right light is critical, but what's the right light? It depends on what you're doing. The different activities that take place in the bedroom require differing intensities and qualities of light.

For example, we need:

- an honest light (perhaps sunlight) for dressing and applying makeup
- a comfortable, direct, glare-free light for reading and game playing
- an indirect light to offset the flashing, flickering TV or computer screen
- a gentle, almost mysteriously soft light for ambience and romance
- adjustable wall spotlights to highlight any feature of the room
- concealed strip lighting fitted around the room's circumference for atmospheric, indirect lighting

*Comfortable lighting:
Recessed ceiling lights
give overall
illumination; swing-
arm lamps on the
window seats give
reading and
atmospheric light;
night-table lamps give
direct or romantic light.
All are on dimmers.*

Design by Samuel Botero
Associates; photography by
Dennis Krukowski.

Think about your light needs before you act automatically to install the usual lamps.

One caveat: I can't imagine living in *any* room, but especially the voluptuous bedroom, without dimmers. It is possible to transform the entire comfort level of a room by the mere flick of a dimmer, easily attached to every artificial light source.

WINDOW LIGHT

Thinking about artificial light makes us also think about bedroom window treatments and we will consider those more fully in chapter VII, "Feathering Your Nest." Generally, however, the following rules ring true:

Blackout shades to control the amount of natural light entering your bedroom can be used with almost any style of window treatment. Make sure they overlap the windowsill and cover the cracks at the side of the window to prevent *any* light from filtering through.

Window treatments should reflect the decorating signature of the rest of the room and also your common sense. You aren't going to achieve a traditional French bedroom look with plastic miniblinds: French calls for swags and tassels. You will also not find a country bedroom in silk or satin drapes (use cotton, organdy, or chintz) or a contemporary look with balloons of cabbage-rose chintz (use chic shades, transparent "throws," or nothing).

Do I have to say it? Comfortable design insists that you don't put a piano in front of the window drapery pull cord so that opening and closing the curtains becomes a daily project. *Unfetter* your bedroom.

MAGIC OF TOUCH, CALM OF FRAGRANCE

The messages we receive through our senses give us information about our world.

As every sensualist knows, there is nothing so emotionally satisfying as fabric that is lovely and comforting to the touch in a room with a fresh and pleasing scent. If your bedroom chaise is charmingly upholstered in starched, crisp organdy that is much too starched and crisp to be body-calming, you have a look-at-me chaise, not a pleasurable, functional chaise, and your sense of tranquillity will be damaged. If your flooring is scratchy or cold, if your blanket is heavy and lumpy, if your desk yields splinters—you will feel annoyingly uncomfortable.

COMFORTING FABRICS

Lush cashmere throws, pliant, downy pillows, velvety chairs, satiny sheets, heated blankets, at-the-ready feet coverlets—name your fabric but *feel* it before you buy it because in any room of the house, but especially your bedroom, fabrics that don't refresh your body and spirit are useless, off-putting and, worse, pretentious.

AROMATHERAPY

There's an ancient science that's gaining new respect called "aromatherapy." The use of fragrance for psychological and physiological healing has always gentled troubled people and induced feelings of well-being and solace. No wonder: The sense of smell is the most experienced of all senses. The nose knows.

Think about it: Sight functions only in light; there are periods when the ear listens but hears nothing; taste sleeps most of the time; and touch requires your cooperation—you have to reach out to feel. But night or day, there is no odorless place for the sensitive nose, and the sense of smell is the most enduring of all senses, often lasting as long as we last. It makes sense to make sure your bedroom is *comfortable* to the nose.

Essential oils or potent plant extracts can contain hormones, vitamins, and fragrance. They can be inhaled through air diffusers, absorbed through facial masks and massage, or simply smelled. Try:

- chamomile compresses to soothe inflammation
- clove ointments to gentle pain
- citrus massages to stimulate digestion

Since fragrance enhances lifestyle in real and subtle ways, care must be taken to avoid an overbearing presence of dirty linen, overstarched bedding, or damp clothes in the laundry basket. Sweet, spicy, or fruity potpourri (depending on preference) in exquisite containers does wonders to enhance an atmosphere. Many people love a fragrant candle for its flickering-light atmosphere as well as its scent.

THERE IS SOMETHING ABOUT GREEN

Plants—fresh, alive, and verdant—are nature's accessories. They add height, color, variety, camouflage, and drama to the bedroom—but, still, most people opt to put greenery in the living room rather than the bedroom. Big mistake. It is somehow reassuring to wake in the morning and see—a tree, right in your very own bedroom.

Of course, greenery needn't be confined to trees. An increasingly wide range of flowering plants is available for the bedroom, and they add romance and even a feeling of wellness. Everyone knows how therapeutic gardening can be—even the indoor variety.

Here are some things to note about bedroom greenery:

- For rich, full growth, most plants need light, warmth, and humidity in varying degrees: Make friends with your florist and get clear directions for green care.
- Greenery must be alive. This sounds simplistic, but plants with sad, brown leaves and trees with decaying blossoms are downright depressing. Don't identify with the plant if it's barely alive: When it's time to get rid of it, close your heart and make it history.
- One abundant, flourishing plant will always have more panache than a collection of struggling ones.
- There's nothing more charming than a sunny windowsill lined with a row of geraniums or daffodils in clay pots.
- Place a large, leafy plant in the corner of a room and then shine a light up through its leaves to make the corner "disappear" and create delicate and mysterious patterns on walls and ceilings.
- The sense of comfort a giant pot of lemon scented–leaved geraniums provides is unparalleled and indescribable.

- A sophisticated bedroom looks stunning with one fabulous orchid plant on a Lucite stand. (Note that orchids don't do well near drafts.) Cut field flowers are delicious for less formal rooms. Dyed daisies and gladioli don't look good anywhere.
- Containers are key: Three pink tulips in a green plastic pot are boring. A dozen pink tulips in a turn-of-the-century pitcher are fabulous.
- Who says a bedroom can't have an *inside* window box filled with greenery of the season?
- Fresh flowers on the night table are romance incarnate.
- If you dislike window treatments but want some privacy, hang plants in baskets in front of the windowpanes. On a wooden or brass pole, hang the baskets in either uniform or varying lengths (for a staggered effect) from chains.
- Do without greenery rather than have a fake ficus tree.

BUT WHAT DO WE DO WITH THE TELEVISION?

The problem of the television never goes away. Far from the prettiest piece of furniture in the world, it is nevertheless a twentieth-century staple, and it almost always lives in the bedroom. But for many of us, the bedroom is no longer a place of isolation.

"Come in, sit down, be welcome in our private turf," we say to our friends on Academy Award night and, friendly as lapdogs, they do.

So where to put the television so everyone can see and it doesn't stick out like a sore thumb? Some suggestions:

- Hide it in one side of the closed armoire so it's invisible when not in use. Inside the armoire, it can rest on a simple carpenter-built swivel base that pulls out and turns so your lapdogs can all have a great view of the Oscar winners.
- Set it into a thick wall or a wall that encroaches on a closet in the next room so it's flush with the wall and nicely out of the way.
- Have a low cabinet built at the foot of the bed and place the television in the cabinet—but on a pop-up shelf for viewing. When it's not in use, the set pops down and is hidden under the lid, with maybe a great, comfy cashmere throw on top.
- Consider some of the newer television stands that are sculptural shapes, antique wrought iron, or Lucite cubes. They are decent alternatives to the "hide it" solution.

Use your common sense: A client of mine, whose television rested on a TV table, loved to watch from her bed. Her husband sat in his adjacent club chair with his feet propped on the bed, obscuring her view of the screen. She bought him an ottoman—but to no avail: He liked the height of the bed for his long legs. For ten years, his wife watched television through her husband's toes. One day, her neighbor discarded a much higher television stand; my client retrieved it, placed her own set on its surface. *Miracle of miracles*—she could finally see the whole screen. No toes. Sometimes solutions come simply.

THE BODY SENSUAL: THE EXERCISE SPA

Attention must be paid to the body as well as the spirit. When we feel limber, strong, and lithe, we feel comfortable and sensual in our skins. This may well explain the explosion of gyms in the health-conscious nineties.

This exercise spa is made personal with the addition of fine art, but it is state-of-the-art high function. It incorporates mirrors for self-monitoring, a television comfortably placed for easy viewing, and the latest equipment.

Design by Teri Seidman Interiors; photography by Bill Rothschild.

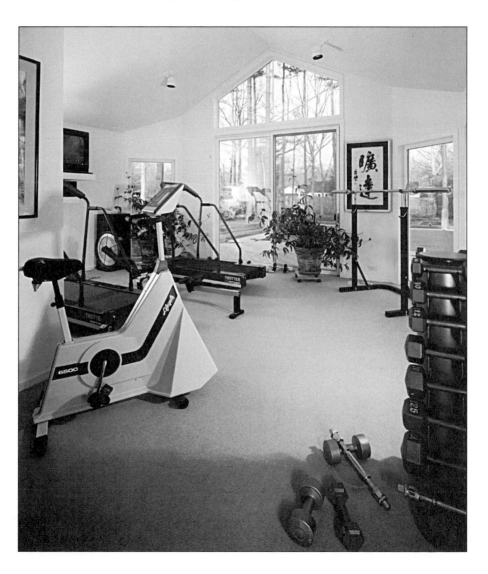

And, as we burrow deeper into our own homes, more of us want our private health spas—right here under our noses.

When space is a problem, many set up mini-exercise spas in a corner of the bedroom; others carve workout areas into the bathroom or home office. However, if you're lucky enough to have a separate small room off the bedroom available, that's the most self-pampering way to go! Here's what you need for the exercise spa:

- a place with nonslip floors (well-sanded wood, cork, or rubber are great), rounded edges, and a floor mat for floor exercises
- a wall of mirrors—preferably several walls—to see yourself coming and going for workouts (it's a good idea to visit several health clubs as a "prospective member," checking out the mirror arrangements to see which feels best to you)
- good ventilation (a window or an air-conditioner, whichever you prefer) is a necessity and if you require privacy, think about appropriate window treatments
- your favorite workout equipment—treadmill, exercise bicycle, stair stepper, Nautilus equipment—all belong in your exercise spa. If you do use a portion of another room for a spa, since it's no fun to set up and dismantle equipment daily, try to find space where the equipment can be permanently set up.
- a surface for the music equipment—the tape deck, radio, or VCR with the exercise video—that encourages you to greater achievement
- book/newspaper holders that attach to exercise equipment are a good comfort touch. Many of us, bored silly with exercise, like to read as we move. Most sporting-goods stores carry them.

THE GUEST BEDROOM

The quintessential host is thoughtful. The bedroom she provides for sleep-overs doesn't have to be enormous, but it should be a place where a guest is moved to sigh with pleasure.

The sensual appeals are what count most: Your guests should be immune to harsh sounds and unpleasant fragrances. They should have good things to touch and see and even taste. They should feel voluptuously comfortable. How to do this?

Walls can be covered with fabric or grass cloth to keep out noise.

Even a small twin bed can be topped with a wonderful, silky antique quilt.

The floor should be warm to the touch.

A rocker is user-friendly.

If the room is furnished with attic leftovers, be sure they're freshly painted so they look charming, not rusty.

A plate of fruit or cookies, a carafe of water, bottled juices, or soda, and an ice bucket are appreciated more than you'd think.

Fresh flowers, extra blankets and pillows, a small radio or TV, a clock, ashtrays for smokers, books, and a stash of magazines are all comfort touches.

Stock adjoining guest bathrooms with:

- fresh toothpaste, toothbrushes, mouthwash, and razors
- sample-sized bottles of shampoo and conditioner
- fresh, wonderful soaps—*always* a fresh bar, as even a little-used soap is gauche
- a small bottle of antacid
- aspirin
- clean towels—not the tiny guest assortment but plush, large, absorbent towels
- a magazine rack with bathroom reads

Social comfort: the easy life with friends and family . . .   Design by Richard Mervis Design, Inc.; photography by Michael Rogol.

IV

SOCIAL COMFORT

....

How many desolate creatures on the earth
Have learnt the simple dues of fellowship
And social comfort . . . ?

—ELIZABETH BARRETT BROWNING

The living room looks like World War III.

Your interesting new neighbors have dropped in to talk but somehow, even though there are only seven adults in the room, you're spread out all over the place—and conversation seems to have come to a dead halt. The stereo is on the floor where it usually lives. The coffee table is covered with papers, so the only place to put drinks is on the floor—and, you've got it: Two drinks have already spilled and are now sopping into your gorgeous white carpet. Crumbs and smoked salmon inhabit the couch because your husband has placed his canapé-topped napkin on the couch arm, for which act you will later kill him.

The family has been trained to stash board games in the corner of the room, but no one's very neat about it so pieces of Trivial Pursuit, three checkers, and a Get Out of Jail Free card (not to mention your son's guitar) are scattered about.

What's more, the room doesn't look pretty or comfortable. The chairs are lumpy, the sofa's too small, and there isn't a hint of greenery for relief.

The dining room is worse. You bring your neighbors in for some coffee and cake, and they sit around your enormous table (you can easily serve fourteen for dinner), stiff-backed, suddenly formal. The artificial-flower arrangement in the center of the table blocks everyone's view of one another. Again, conversation falters. You notice, as your heart sinks, that the wax flowers are dusty. Also ugly.

Worst of all, trying to see the dining and living rooms through your guests' eyes, it's suddenly clear that you live in a *boring* place. For starters, there's no piece of furniture or view special enough on which to rest your attention. Nothing about the rooms gives clues to what interesting people *you* are. Furniture seems, well, lined up, and although you chose each piece for its beauty, suddenly none seems welcoming or cozy. Your guests fidget—not too surprising since even you feel vaguely ill at ease, and you live here.

Soon, your neighbors leave, walking quickly back through your dark front hall.

How embarrassing.

It doesn't take a rocket scientist to see that your home's not heavy in social comforts.

What to do? Start by getting rid of the guitar and the games in the living room? Absolutely not. The very first doctrine of comfort decorating is to claim, not hide, your personal identity. Homes should say, "I work here, play here, eat here. . . ." and ways must be found to acknowledge your life-style, accentuate its unique qualities, give it space to breathe and grow, not shove it in a hidden corner. Signs of you, shades of your personality in every room are precisely what gives your home character and appeal. Careful planning can accomplish this and still let you have a beautiful, controlled design umbrella.

For example: Your son plays and practices his guitar in the dining room:

A wall unit can be built to house and actually display his guitar—really a beautiful thing to see, as interesting and spiraling in design as the most superb Brancusi sculpture.

Depending on the style of your design umbrella, an exquisite antique wooden music stand or one made of sleek, shining chrome can be given prominence in one area of the room that has been artfully separated from the actual dining space.

Because all decorating is about relationships, the shape and the colors in the instrument can be echoed in freestanding or wall artwork.

Depending on your chosen style, sheet music and other hobby accoutrements can be stowed away in a formal armoire or a charming painted chest that also serves as home to cutlery and napkins.

Another example: You love to sew and do needlepoint. Your living room is a morass of spools, needles, and skeins of yarn. Here again, declare your unique self but do it beautifully and with control:

Set aside a corner of your living room so that you and your guests can be comfortable even as you're surrounded with expressions of your life-style. Instead of painting or papering the whole living room, line one corner with a needlepoint-like fabric that complements the colors and style of the rest of the room. This touch alone sets off your corner from the rest of the room, even as it blends in nicely.

Give a portion of the wall over to a display of antique or modern spools—a wall of embroidery/sculptural shapes.

Haunt antique stores for appropriate furniture you can convert to your own use. A turn-of-the-century sewing machine stand and seat can make a wonderful coffee table or plant stand. A magnificent, carved-wood dentist's cabinet from the same era—the kind with myriad drawers—can hold your sewing supplies and also serve as storage for coasters, cocktail napkins, and family games.

Celebrate yourself—don't try to conceal your spirit. Social comfort is defined by signs of real life: Go for it in your decorating!

First step: Determine all the functions of each room.

COMFORT ZONE CHECKLIST: THE LIVING ROOM

CONVERSATIONAL AND ACTIVITY COMFORT

Picture your living room filled with as many people as you *usually* have in that room. It is for this number you will design the room. Forget your fantasy of twenty people happily chatting away; instead, think, how often do twenty people chat in your living room? Decorate for reality, not for magazine images.

What do you usually *do* in your living room? Do you always use it as a family room or do you most often use it for guests? Do your children play in the living room, do you ever eat meals, drink, exercise, do hobbies, listen to or play music, sew or knit, nap, watch television, read, or work in the living room? What do you usually store in this room?

Do you usually prefer to have your guests involved in one conversation, or do you find that your guests generally break into more than one conversational group?

FEET-UP COMFORT

Is the seating (or lounging around) designed for bodies or for mannequins? Will you need at least one wonderful club chair, chaise longue, or sink-in sofa?

How are you fixed for ottomans or surfaces on which to put feet?

ENTERTAINING EASE

Decide on the approximate number of surfaces you'll need on which to place drinks, food, books, games: Remember that every seating cluster ought to have a nearby and accessible surface.

Do you need *storage* for your social comforts, i.e., a place to keep coasters, glasses, liquor, napkins? What about storage for the living-room games you play—backgammon, cards, Trivial Pursuit? What about extra chairs or snack tables? It's wonderful not to have to dig out these items from the backs of dark, crowded closets.

Do you do the type of entertaining that would be comfortably served by a bar right in the living room?

COMFORTABLE TRAFFIC FLOWS

Think about the games you play, the views you need (of the television, the outdoors), your comfortable access to doors, switches, window shades. Can guests (and your family) move easily around the room without falling over one another or the furniture?

Can you figure out how to place your furniture in clusters that don't impede traffic flow?

Can you figure out how to create cozy nooks and crannies so people can comfortably conduct different activities at the same time—without interfering with each other?

ELECTRONIC COMFORT

Will you need a place in which to sink your stereo/television (if you don't have a separate media room)? Do you need advice on where to place speakers for maximum effect?

What kind of lighting do you need or feel most comfortable with in the living room? Reading lights? Atmosphere or ambient lighting? Focus or task lights?

VISUAL COMFORTS

Is there a definite focal point, a place where the natural attention of the room is first focused—like a magnificently tiled fireplace or a marvelous view of city or country?

Will you want to display art or bibelots that express your individuality? What about wall and table surfaces for these?

Will you want the center of attraction to be a potpourri of *many* interesting or beautiful things to look at? Or will you want center stage to belong to one startling or beautiful large object like an Oriental carpet or a wall-storage unit? Or do you love a room that's a masterpiece of understatement and simplicity?

COMFORT ZONE CHECKLIST: THE LIVING ROOM

How about art? Have you thought about eclectic and unusual? Originals or reproductions? Do you prefer simple—or controlled profusion? What about the architectural proportions of the furniture to go in this living room? Is everything you already own too high? Too low? What will you need to buy to balance the proportions? How can you use the natural architecture of the living room to create an elegant symmetry?

Now, begin to decorate for social comfort.

BUT FIRST, WELCOME HOME

THE FRONT DOOR

How nice to get a feeling of welcome, a sense of sociable ease, before one even opens the front door. The feel of the doorknob in your hand often sets the stage for what's to come.

Many styles to complement your design umbrella are available, but when choosing a new outer doorknob, I'll always opt for the comfort of the graceful, soft, almost feminine egg-shaped doorknob, which feels just right in the hand. The egg has some bulk to it as befits an outer door, but it also has a sensual grace that the traditional round knob lacks. The egg is available in traditional brass, but more contemporary brass and chrome or chrome and black metal finishes are also options.

THE FRONT HALL

For your family as well as for guests, nothing sets the scene for social comfort so much as the first place you see: the entranceway. The front hall marks the boundary between the impersonal world and someone's personal haven. It is a transition from the cold to the warm: It tells you you're home safe. The entranceway may be very spacious and grand, but for a feeling of safety, it needs to be intimate. That's why large halls are best zoned into smaller, cozy welcome spaces.

In order to experience a clear difference between outside and inside, one must feel immediately cushioned upon entering. The front hall is also the place to rest for a second before moving on to the rich interior life of the rest of the house. This is where one can pause, put down packages or keys, get rid of a coat, and check the mirror.

Think of the front hall as a small room—even though no one stays there long. Its decoration should definitely introduce your design umbrella: Furniture, mirrors, or art should signal what's to come. If your decor is country, for example, try an antique English country coatrack in your front

The front hall sets the first and last impressions of home . . . in this case, Classic Americana.   Courtesy of F. Schumacher & Co.

The truly welcoming *front hall* always *offers a table on which to drop keys or parcels and a mirror to check one's appearance. This Fine Traditional front hall is neoclassical.*

Design by Stephen Mallory Associates; photography by Kari Haavisto.

A *front hall that signals a Regional Flair–Adirondack design umbrella.*

Design by Ronald Bricke & Associates, Inc.; photography by Michael Hill.

hall, or large, Shaker-inspired wall hooks, or even a wonderful knotty-pine armoire in which to hang coats and hats. Umbrella stands should be beautiful as well as functional, and remember the exquisitely framed mirror: People like to reassure themselves about their appearance as they enter.

A welcoming surface on which to place things is so important, but a small, beautiful table can also display the things you love—if you also leave room for its primary purpose.

Flooring is key to comfort: Surfaces should be pretty but durable. No one should have to worry about tracking in dirt, so even if your entire home is carpeted wall to wall, a pretty mat in the front hall is appreciated. Even better than carpeting are defined marble, tile, or wood areas for entranceways.

Good light is essential. The only thing as depressingly uncomfortable as a uniformly dark, somber entranceway is one that is floodlit to the hilt. Soft, natural light is best, but a right-by-the-door switch that turns on gentle artificial light also turns on an interior welcome.

CONVERSATIONAL EASE

As people begin to come home again and comfortably "nest in" with friends, they often go first to the living room. In past decades, the living room was the formal, look-at-me place where people sat gingerly and talked politely. Today, the living room has come into its own as the place where people most vitally *live*—that is, where they relax, share their secrets, their plans, their politics, their very essence. The living room has become *the* place to *talk*.

Years ago, Dr. Edward Hall, a social behaviorist, conducted a celebrated study of people's use of space between their bodies in different situations. He came to the conclusion that

- lovers were most comfortable talking to each other at a distance of 6 to 18 inches.
- two *very* good friends dealt best when chatting at $1^1/_2$ to $2^1/_2$ feet apart.
- absolute strangers were not comfortable when there was less than 12 to 15 feet between them.
- at a gathering in someone's living room, people felt most comfortable conversing at what Dr. Hall defined as social space—4 to 12 feet apart.

Think of the implications of Dr. Hall's social space. Five friends enter your living room. If, in this living room, there is a traditional three-seater sofa flanked by three beautiful chairs, each placed about 13 feet from the other, technically there will be room for all of you to sit comfortably and chat—right?

Heirloom quilts, a blazing fire, a tray of tea and cookies on a companionable surface make for Tranquil Country conversation.

Design by Ronald Bricke & Associates, Inc.; photography by Michael Hill.

Wrong. When was the last time you saw someone willingly sit in the center of a three-person couch? It doesn't happen, except in times of dire need. I call it The Seat of Last Resort. There's no place to put your arms, no place to put your drink, it's too close to talk comfortably with those on either side, and you have to keep turning your head to do that anyway. It's just plain uncomfortable. The ones who get the beautiful chairs aren't comfortable either, even the guest on your magnificent eighteenth-century Federal "easy" chair. For starters, the easy chair's not the slightest bit easy, and everyone is too far from the couch and each other for conversational ease; your guests find they have to raise their voices and lean forward to one another in order to shorten some of the uncomfortable distance that separates them.

SEATING SOLUTIONS

- Don't ever count a three-seater sofa as a three-seater.
- Think of how people *gather*—and create several natural gathering places instead of sterile seating places. Visualize the gathering places as small islands within the larger room.

Consider the following configurations:

- two love seats facing each other with one or two easy chairs on their periphery
- two small couches, or a couch and a love seat, facing each other or at right angles to each other—and a sink-into-me chaise flanking the couches at an attractive angle
- two distinctly different conversational areas: two sofas, placed back to back with comfortable chairs around each sofa
- a modular couch that swings companionably around a corner. Face the couch with a plush club chair.
- open, U-shaped sitting areas work conversational miracles for both small and large crowds

Note: Contemporary-design sofas are looser, larger, more comfortable than ever before. Some wonderful versions even extend by pressing a button for feet-up comfort—not like an inexpensive lounger chair but by remaining their own, elegant selves, only slightly longer. They come in everything from slouchy, kid-glove-soft leathers to indestructible cottons. In fact, there's a distinct move from apparel fabrics to furnishings; the very fabrics we enjoy wearing when we're away from the workplace are showing up on sofas. And they wear like a good pair of jeans, getting softer and more natural with age—which makes denim a popular choice. Traditional sofas in more formal fabrics can entertain in elegant style and still retain deep, clubby comfort: The secret lies in plumping up the volume with plushy pillows. Try:

- a giant floor pillow, compatible with your decor, as extra floor seating for the young or agile
- a cushion on the Federal easy chair

FURNITURE: THE SHAPE OF COMFORT

Furniture comfort comes to us through the body, the way it feels—but also through the eye, the way it looks: the generous proportions and warm patina of a wall-sized mahogany bookcase, the folds of soft leather on a contemporary sofa, an overstuffed Victorian armchair with its deeply tufted rich fabrics and lace antimacassars.

One very large coffee table can be the epitome of serving ease—as well as a giant display place for precious keepsakes that make a home comfortably personal.

Design by Barbara Ostrom; photography by Bill Rothschild.

➤ A stack of fine, fat floor pillows is comfort.
➤ Loosely covered, unmatched armchairs are comfort.
➤ Generous surface space is comfort.

SURFACES

See that there are accessible, comfortable surfaces—a coffee table, end table, ottoman, in-back-of-the-sofa table, or another usable surface that serves each seating area. As people talk, they need to do something with their hands, which usually means sipping a drink or juggling a plate of canapés that needs a resting place.

TIPS

- Opt for one large or several small coffee tables: No one should have to fight for space.
- Choose tables that aren't flimsy or easily damaged—it may not be the height of social decorum, but real people often put their feet up on the coffee table.
- Think about good-looking nesting tables for coffee (or occasional) tables to ensure flexibility in your living room. People in the heat of conversation *often* rearrange your furniture, pulling their own chairs and movable tables closer to another person or even to the warmth

Lavish fringed detail, lush fabric, crushable throw pillows combine for a club chair and matching ottoman of incomparable peace.

Design by Barbara Ostrom; photography by Bill Rothschild.

of a fireplace. Consider this a tribute to your plan for social comfort, because when people follow their own instincts, and you are flexible enough to rearrange on the spot, everyone's happy. Pull-up tables lend spontaneity to conversational ease.

UPHOLSTERED COMFORT

Although a pair of delicate painted side chairs or a willowy rosewood settee may be grace notes under your design umbrella, for most people the essence of comfort derives from coverings and cushions, stuffings and springs—the art of upholstery. Here are the classics in upholstered furniture.

THE CLUB CHAIR

Sometimes called "Daddy's Chair," the club chair is Mommy's, yours, and mine also. It shelters, rises up around the sitter, and permits her to chat, doze, have a drink, hold a book or a baby—in other words, although it doesn't move, you can: The club chair encourages you to shift positions to whatever is comfortable. You sit in a club chair—not on it. It comes plushly upholstered and it loves an ottoman.

THE CHAISE

One or more chaises longues can double as sofas or be paired with other furniture. Depending on your decorating style, living-room chaises come in sleek leathers, charming chintzes, rich tapestries, and many other upholstered choices. They are the heart of comfort.

THE MOTION CHAIR

The ability to change body posture as one relaxes has a true social function, says Witold Rybczynksi in his classic book, *Home.* Some chairs should actually help you express body language, let you lean forward (to express interest or concern), or recline backward (to indicate relaxation or pensiveness).

The motion chair, or recliner, is steeped in nostalgic associations—none of them having to do with fine design. A few years ago, it was an ungainly piece of furniture traditionally confined to the den or hidden in a living-room corner—the chair on which Dad watched the football game and Mom knit yet another sweater. It seemed the essence of comfort, but ugly comfort. In fact, the recliner had become something of a cliché whose reputation was lumped right up there with Spam, Cool Whip, and mobile homes. The good news? The recliner has been brought back. True comfort never goes out of style for long. The La-Z-Boy's inventors would feel happy to know that recliners have become de rigueur for a New Age generation come home again; these grown-up baby boomers now think that reclining and rocking chairs are cool and even therapeutic.

There is a host of new designs available, ranging from the classic Eames chair to the really new "lounge" chairs and even the redesigned rocking chair (wonderful in traditional country wood, but just as wonderful in contemporary steel). The motion lounge chair doesn't even look like a recliner anymore. It comes in the guise of a beautiful club chair, wing chair, or chaise longue. In leather or in bold graphics or elegant European fabrics, some recliners have drop-down tables, telephone compartments, and convenient hidden storage spaces. They can even be in the very latest high-tech design: Ferdinand Porsche, for example, designed a black leather recliner with a sculptured aluminum channeled frame that is marked by the same craftsmanship and style that distinguishes his automobiles.

The ultimate in comfortable recliners is Hammacher Schlemmer's version, which gives a *shiatsu* massage.

THE PERFECT SOFA

The living room is often defined by its largest piece of furniture, and usually that is the sofa. Impossible to hide, full of intricate secrets, the wrong sofa can be a terrible frustration. One must choose a sofa carefully: It's bigger than a roommate and harder to get rid of.

First of all, the perfect sofa must protect and shelter. Some people like high-backs, which are psychologically comforting, a concept harking back to the days when people felt safer if their backs were protected. Others prefer free-form, low-backed sofas. Some like extra-deep sofas, deep enough for snoozing. Everyone likes a sofa that's pleasant to the touch.

Beauty is not only skin deep. To find the perfect sofa, one must get to know its character and background and check its references. These are the qualities to look for:

- From the myriad of stylistic choices available, try to select a sofa with a solid, single hardwood frame (like maple or birch) that contracts and expands as the weather changes so the frame won't weaken or creak. The frame should also be padded for ultimate comfort. How much padding? Squeeze the arms and back of the sofa: The less frame you feel, the better.

- Long, graceful curves and other generous proportions are expensive to manufacture and thus indicate high quality.

- Traditional sofas should have good suspension systems with hand-tied coil springs. Contemporary sofas, more sculptural in shape, may be constructed with ribbons of continuous flat coils or four-way stretch-webbing systems. Nonelastic, interwoven webbing is *not* a comfortable suspension system.

- Lift the sofa at one end. If it feels absurdly light or if it wiggles or sags or creaks as it's being raised, think again before purchasing it.

- Sofa cushions should fit the frame without gaps or overcrowding,

Pure comfort protects and shelters. This inviting sofa is served by a go-anywhere table on which to snack or play.

Design by Barbara Ostrom; photography by Phillip H. Ennis.

and they should be padded and filled with multiple layers of batting material—not a thin layer of inferior-cut foam or polyester batting. Polyurethane foam (at least 1.8 pounds per cubic foot—ask your salesman to supply the density statistics) is fine padding. A really great sofa cushion, however, will be filled with 80 percent goose down and 20 percent good feathers: The less down in the cushions, the less luxuriously comfortable the sofa will be.

❧ Finally, sit on the sofa, plop down on it! Experts recommend you stay put for five minutes, paying particular attention to the sofa's ability to support your back without pitching you forward, like the backseat of a convertible does.

SOFA SELLING POINTS:

Choose your sofa fabric for comfort and durability—not just good looks. For example, vinyl sticks to the body, wool can scratch and feel hot in the summertime, and certain inexpensive synthetics (like olefin) feel slithery to the touch. Test large swatches of a chosen fabric on your skin for comfort before making a final decision.

Make sure the sofa seat is not so low and deep that you have trouble rising from it.

Everyone in your family should try out the sofa before the final purchase.

FOOTSTOOLS

Traditional ottomans or a variety of hassocks, miniature chaises, or children's chairs, large pillows, and other feet-up pieces make every big armchair a personal oasis of comfort. Think of it this way: A footstool is whatever raises the legs from the floor and encourages you to catch some z's.

TIP: *Maintenance Magic:* If any of your furniture is constructed of hardwood, for your own comfort and for the long life of the hardwood, consider using a humidifier to keep relative humidity at 25 percent to 35 percent. Solid hardwood furniture always retains some moisture and in your home the wood continues to shrink and expand in response to changes in the humidity. For this reason, also avoid placing hardwood furniture directly in front of radiators.

The warmth of an ottoman can be transformed into a functional coffee table.

Design by Anne Mullin Interiors for Kip's Bay; photography by Peter Vitale.

CREATURE COMFORTS: THE PLAY FACTOR

Some of us are lucky enough to have special media or family rooms particularly designed for ease of entertainment, and we will talk about these later. There are still many of us, however, who wish to use our living rooms for play.

Do you often entertain guests around the television set at Oscar/Emmy awards, Super Bowls, or tennis tournaments?

Do you use your living-room VCR for rented movie parties for friends or family?

Do you have regular musicales around the piano or do you invite the viola-da-gamba group over to practice on a regular basis?

Would a bar add to your entertaining ease?

Whether play is centered around a grand piano or a magnificent backgammon or chess table, putting our hobbies up front conveys what we're about to the rest of the world. We're embracing and displaying our playful sides instead of hiding them.

The way to decorate around the play factor is to create small islands of activity: We call it "zoning."

Separate your living room into different areas where one member of the family can hold court with friends around the backgammon table while other members can sew in another corner. Use screens, area rugs or furniture to delineate the zones which, taking the same cues for colors and fabrics, should be linked together under one design umbrella.

THE GREEN FACTOR

Green is the great equalizer inside as well as outside. There is something about the energetic, crisp shades of greenery that refreshes the spirit. Greens act as relaxing and peaceful coolants when added to warm rooms; ironically, they rarely make cooler rooms feel cold, since they are such a natural background color to living things. Living greenery blends with and actually enhances every other color in the room.

Potted plants and fresh flowers are wonderful additions, especially to a living room—if you *keep* them green and healthy. They seem to boost sociability and good cheer. Leafy foliage also softens hard furniture lines and walls. Lush trees in huge porcelain pots can also serve as screens or dividers when you want to zone off an area. Dull windowsills can be used for greenhouse stages, enlivening the view.

Flowers should always be fresh or dried, never wax, and silk only if they're magnificent—and magnificent silk flowers are always expensive.

Greenery Tips

Containers

Plastic saucers and tubs that look for all the world as though they were clay can be found at the better florist shops. Benefit: they don't leak, as clay sometimes does. A classic choice for indoor plants is called the "Versailles" planter—white wood with a rigid waterproof liner. Ornamental containers of every variety can be planted directly or used as cachepots to hide ugly pots.

Placement

Don't confine greenery to one level. Interest and a sense of height derive from tall, stately plants; intimacy and closer appreciation come from eye-level greenery and cut flowers.

A room can be given a sense of depth and perspective as well as height by adding a screen and placing a table, a large plant, and a painting on an easel.

Exaggeration is a simple and often inexpensive way to lend drama to room style. Placing four charmingly potted red geranium plants right near a striking poster of a giant red geranium can be beautiful as well as a conversation starter.

A boring corner turns distinguished when filled with a fruit-laden miniature orange tree.

Grouped in twos and threes, different heights of the same plant (like dracaenas) look marvelous against a brick fireplace during the summer months.

Hanging plants can be trailed down an otherwise uncovered window, and "creepers" like ivy or jasmine can easily be grown up an inside wall for a delightful effect.

A living room *profuse* in greenery creates an instant garden room that smells like summer even when the snow falls: On the mantel, on desks, as a table centerpiece—the green factor fits anywhere.

Kinds of Plants for Indoors

Most indoor plants thrive best in temperatures between 55 and 75 degrees. Hardy ones like ivy and aspidistra tolerate temperatures as low as 40 degrees—perfect for windowsills. Others like ferns and begonias won't thrive at all below 50 degrees.

Spray plants more in the winter when central heating pervades the atmosphere and lukewarm-water them more frequently. *Caveat:* Some plants need to dry out totally between waterings, and others need to be kept perennially moist. Ask when you buy.

The following plants or trees are notable for their foliage, flowers, or both:

Lemon scented–leaved geraniums; geraniums come in myriad forms besides the standard window-box variety, and they are among the hardiest and prettiest of flowering plants.

Intensely colored primulas make a room come alive!

Fuchsias in varied combinations of pink, red, orange, purple, and white are delightful in imaginative containers.

Gardenia plants: Not the easiest to bring to flower indoors but their smooth, creamy blooms and heady fragrance are worth the effort!

The ubiquitous ficus tree does very well indoors and its graceful, delicate leaves are not overbearing in a smaller room.

Philodendron laciniatum—a hardy, pretty leaf.

Don't ignore your design umbrella when choosing greenery. You don't have to be obsessive about this. Any lovely greenery or blooms complement almost every look. Still, some choices are defining! For example:

A Sleek Contemporary room could be smashing with an orchid plant, one stark white lily, or an exotic palm tree as an accessory.

Tranquil Country looks delightful with flats of daffodils, blooming hyacinths, or a lacy lavender plant lending an old-fashioned potpourri scent.

For a Fine Traditional living room, think of paperwhite narcissus or fabulous cabbage roses or a standing fern without which no Victorian parlor was complete.

A Classic Americana living room would be swell with massive amounts of begonias caught in a huge pewter bowl or a Christmas evergreen fern in a copper tub.

And a room steeped in Regional Flair? How about a stunning giant cactus for a deserty atmosphere or a generous jade plant with the naturally picturesque look of a Japanese bonsai tree for a room redolent of the Far East?

Let your imagination run . . .

Details for Realness

Real living rooms must look beautifully used and lived in. Details tell you not only who lives in a home but also who's welcome. Try these details:

- Elegant throws on couches, chairs, or chaises: a rough-edged shearling for an Adirondack living room, a rich tapestry for a European traditional room, a textured needlepoint for a classic country room
- Plush, comfortable pillows tossed on chairs and couches for comfort and color contrast, ranging from traditional tapestries to geometric jacquards for a contemporary dash
- Rich pattern-on-pattern surprises: mixes of paisleys, florals, checks, and stripes sharing variations of the same color palettes

Details make a room your very own. Richly patterned pillows, tasseled trims, finely framed photographs, and carefully chosen flowers and greenery personalize this room. The varied patterns work well together because they share common colors.

Design by Jamie Gibbs & Associates; photography by Bill Rothschild.

- A profusion of personal details to etch your image in the room: travel treasures, antique picture frames, books, collections
- Artwork: "found treasures" displayed on walls and tables, original paintings, framed children's art propped up against or hanging on walls
- Symmetry for serenity and harmony: High style and deep club comfort can entertain in the same room. The secret is to keep a dynamic balance.
- Nonglare surfaces: Spray glass with nonglare solution or redistribute artificial lighting to provide tranquil ambience.

- Check noise levels: Jarring, reverberating outside noises are not peaceful when they enter your living room. Check ceiling acoustics and uncarpeted floors for solutions.
- Finally, for ideas on the details that make a living room comfortable, check your favorite sit-com living room where all of America feels at home. On the *Cosby* show, the Huxtable residence with its ethnic art, sink-in sofas, and ubiquitous throw shawls and pillows reflect the occupants' penchant for family gatherings—as well as sophisticated style and taste. On *The Golden Girls,* the airy living room is filled with rattan furniture and floral cushions—comfort in a sun-drenched, Palm Beach, Florida style. On *Dynasty,* the reproduction Winterthur furniture and the commodious French marble-topped chests represent the comfort of old money. To each his own.

BODY AND SOUL

If comfortable furniture gentles the body, spiritual comforts ease the soul. Some suggestions:
- Books: Line the walls with them. Touch them. Most of all, read them. But even if you don't, just the presence of the written word, the wisdom of the ages, is enough to make one feel comforted.
- Fish Tanks: Ever watch a gold fish for fifteen minutes? Is there anything more relaxing?
- Flowers: Fresh and fragrant. The moment one wilts, out it goes. Nothing is more life-giving than a full-bodied rose, nothing more depressing than a dying one.
- Art: A living room without color, lines, sculpture, or symbols feels unfinished and bare, *un*comfortably sterile.
- Music: Your favorites. Funky or classical, it should be played mellow when guests are present; blaring people out of their socks is not spiritual, unless they like blare.

DINING PLACES

The dining room has come a long way, changing profoundly in character. Today, for most of us, the place where we dine is rarely the formal, proper room where family, friends, or business colleagues are tyrannized by a "matched set" stiffness. We no longer think that sit-up-straight, stilted dining performances are appealing. We even find it impossible to enjoy the food, let alone the company, with such rigid bread-breaking decorum. Ritualized, overformal dining rooms are the very antithesis of decorating for comfort. How can you eat your dripping lobster in such a daunting, starchy dining room?

As we come home again to find our ease, some of us still set aside a whole room, make it as comfortable as it is pretty, and use it just for dining. Many more of us, however, tend to think of the dining room as the Anywhere-You-Find-It Room.

Sometimes we dine in the kitchen, sometimes on the country porch or city terrace, sometimes in a large foyer, sometimes in a corner of the living room, and sometimes in a room that used to be only the dining room but now is a multipurpose room where we watch television, sleep out-of-town guests, hold business conferences—*and* dine. It is a chameleon room, changing its appearance as its purpose changes, and that old formal dining table is now often used to work and play on as well as to eat on.

The fragile-fabric, matched dining chairs have been exchanged for

---

COMFORT ZONE CHECKLIST: THE DINING PLACE

THE TABLE AND CHAIRS

Is your dining table too long, too wide, or too big for conversational ease? Is the table size fixed—that is, it can't be made larger or smaller for entertaining coziness?

Are your dining chairs a matched set of discomfort? Are the seats too low or too high for easy eating? Do you find your guests seem eager to leave the table after finishing the meal? Have you ever considered another type of seating rather than the traditional set of dining room chairs?

How many people usually eat at your table?

Do you eat in several rooms of your home? Are you adequately set up for this?

CONVENIENCE

Are there enough serving surfaces?

Even if it's called the "dining room," are you happy eating there? Or do you find yourself taking most of your meals in another, less formal place because it's more convenient?

Is there enough storage space? Do you have to go into another room or displace your guests to find an extra knife or napkin?

Is it difficult to transport food, dishes, and silverware between table and kitchen?

MOOD AND FLEXIBILITY

Is your dining setting pleasurable? Are there pretty or interesting focal points, architectural details, or decoration where a guest might rest her eyes with interest?

Can your dining area function equally well for a family breakfast as for a formal dinner party?

Does the dining lighting lend itself to your design umbrella? Is it flexible—that is, can you adapt your lighting to lend romance, drama, work comfort, or whatever else you have in mind?

GET REAL

Finally, do you take your *real* dining needs into consideration? Can you beautifully and comfortably serve your family or your friends where you most enjoy eating informally—a bedroom, living room, patio, den—even in a foyer or cozy book-lined niche?

Now, begin to decorate your dining place.

Social comfort: a gently welcoming room for friends to gather in. The bookshelves, art, and antique tapestry screen are a warm backdrop to conversational ease. Intricate layers of print on print are tied together with shared colors.

Design by Teri Seidman Interiors; photography by Bill Rothschild.

*Cozy country: Blue
and white stripes make
chairs, walls, and
windows friendly.
Huge pine surfaces are
laden with country
collections and scones
for tea. A floor-to-
ceiling cabinet is used
for storage and display.
A floral-pillowed
window seat is snugly
placed.*

Design by Diane A. Kovacs
Interior Design, Inc.; photography
by Bill Rothschild.

*Comfort colors:
Tuscany earth tones of
honey, russet, and
apricot (accented by
acid green) prevail. A
neoclassical chaise,
plopped with pillows, is
an elegant stretch-out
corner. A handy surface
and reading light adds
to the comfort. The
window niche is
dramatized by draperies
originally placed for a
softening ambience.*

Design by John Buscarello;
photography by Bill Rothschild.

*Do it with mirrors:
The deft placement of a
mirror to reflect an
outside vista makes a
room appear larger and
prettier.*

Design by John Buscarello;
photography by Bill Rothschild.

A *hearth is the essence of comfort. Primary colors and Fine Traditional accessories combine in a welcoming room.*

Design by Samuel Botero Associates; photography by Phillip H. Ennis.

There's a lot happening
in this room to make it
pure comfort. The
semishelter bed with
plump pillows makes it
a safe haven. The
profusely patterned
rugs warm the floor and
psyche Wall hangings
insulate and protect. A
go-anywhere table is a
handy surface.
Contained clutter
personalizes.

Design by Ken Hockin;
photography by Bill Rothschild.

*White, plump chairs
and a cityscape.*

Design by Joy Mazur Design
Associates, Inc.; photography by
Peter Vitale.

Easygoing seating: A damask banquette embraces a charming dining spot. The round table and pull-up chairs empower conversation.

Design by Sandra Nunnerly; photography by Michael Munday.

A private sanctum: A pillowed window seat invites dreaming. A go-anywhere table invites dining. An antique, gathered-white-silk standing screen invites privacy. Treasured antiques turn formality into livable comfort.

Design by Teri Seidman Interiors; photography by Bill Rothschild.

Just a wall: Cozy is sitting side by side. This intimate spot is balanced with two ancestral portraits, two bronze sconces, and two sink-in silk pillows.

Design by Teri Seidman Interiors; photography by Bill Rothschild.

*C*hairs and fabrics
don't have to match,
but they do have to
relate to the whole
effect. The comfortably
upholstered chairs
relate to the Queen
Anne chairs because
they're all the same
height. Further, the
Queen Anne chairs and
table share the same
wood. Finally, the
floral upholstery on the
chairs echoes the
wallpaper.

Courtesy of F. Schumacher & Co.

hardier versions, including lush club chairs, couches, and banquettes (which can double as sleeping spaces for guests).

The old dining room is the new gathering place that keeps us lingering long after dessert has been served.

So, if the new dining place is anywhere-you-find-it, are there no rules at all? There are.

There is still the formula: *FSC: function, style, comfort.*

Function: Count the number of people who usually use the dining place and determine for what purposes it is used besides dining. For example, you will not need a table for twelve if you have twelve for dinner only twice a year. On the days the twelve do come, your table with leaves can be opened or you can extend your dining capacity by adding one or two beautifully set smaller tables. If your dining-room table is consistently used for work or play, you must guard against choosing one with a fragile finish. Do you have storage problems for the extra bridge chairs you need for a large dinner party? Perhaps you might consider building plush banquette seating around your table—the seats that never have to be stored.

Style: Choose furniture, fabrics, flooring, wallpaper and accessories to fit under your design umbrella.

Comfort: Don't settle for anything that doesn't feel good. If you generally eat in several rooms in your home, perhaps two or three workable dining places are the most logical way to decorate. If you opt for the formal dining room, common sense decrees that it not be situated far from the kitchen. If you fall in love with a set of magnificent Charles II ladder-back dining chairs that kill your back, fall out of love.

THE TRADITIONAL DINING ROOM

Some of us still like to dine, especially when guests are coming, in a special room set aside for the purpose. If we have the space, it's a fine luxury.

THE TABLE: ITS STYLE AND SIZE

The style of your dining room table should fit under your design umbrella: A huge, square glass-and-steel table doesn't support the look of a room that is in every other respect Classic Americana. You can, however, make exceptions according to the 80/20 rule: A room that is 80 percent Americana will support 20 percent worth of glass, steel, or other contemporary touches. Since the table, however, is the very life of the dining room, its style should not depart drastically from the look you've chosen for your design umbrella.

For versatility, many traditional dining tables have always come in flip-top versions, with drop leaves or extensions. Today, the most contemporary designs are flexible: Even glass tables are often designed with extensions, as are high-tech, Italian-born versions with lacquered wings. What's more, a charmingly sized table for six can be made larger even if it doesn't come with extensions: Top it with a large, made-to-order wooden board covered with a smashing tablecloth.

What shape table? A long, narrow table may look very royal, but it will not serve ease of conversation. My dream table is circular, and it happily accommodates six to eight people. Think of it this way: Comfort dining means *dining,* not eating on the run, not grabbing a bite, not getting

A *perfectly comfortable round dining table ringed with fully upholstered armchairs in which to linger after dinner.*
Design by Joy Mazur Design Associates, Inc.; photography by Peter Vitale.

through a meal. The shape of a table can nourish the psyche as efficiently as food nourishes the body. Long, endless tables do not make for intimate comfort dining.

Whatever shape, the table should have room for family-style dining— those in-the-middle-of-the-table platters that invite self-service. It should provide your guests with generous elbowroom, uncramped leg room, and space to push back their chairs.

Finally, surface protection like invisible plastic laminates should be considered, particularly if children dine regularly at your table.

THE CHAIRS: THINK LINGER

Now we're really talking ease: The right dining chairs—padded, uphol-stered, plushed-up—make one wish to linger long after a meal is done.

MIX AND MATCH

Of course, the traditional set of matched dining chairs can still be lovely, but for comfort try mix and match:

- A wingback chair at your dining table? Sure. Where else do you need a couple of hours of sustained comfort more?
- Two club chairs with arms facing each other at your table? If you have the room, they're terrific!
- A couch or a wall banquette (a permanently fixed upholstered bench) servicing one part of the table in addition to four facing chairs? Stretch-out bliss.

In fact, anything is possible, including the mix of traditional, straight-back dining chairs with just one or two living room–type chairs at either end of a rectangular or square table. The secret to *pretty* comfort dining? Different chairs that bear a relationship to one another. Here are some possibilities:

- Unrelated chairs become kissing cousins when they are upholstered in the same fabric
- Unrelated chairs relate if they are identical in height
- Unrelated chairs relate if they are made from very similar woods or metals
- Unrelated chairs relate if at least two "head of the table" chairs are in the same fabric

ANOTHER WAY?

There are even more options to the traditional dining table and chairs. Perhaps *two* small round tables? Or, if a dining room window is the proper height, what about an upholstered window seat to accommodate one side of the table? Only your creative imagination limits the possibilities.

LIGHT UP THE FEAST!

There are many lighting options for the dining room that separately and together can make dining a personal, exciting experience.

Dining in the dark is never comfortable. Romance or drama don't happen when guests have to wonder what they're eating. Instead, try mood lighting. Chandeliers, dimmed to easy ambience, make for a dramatic table. Keep the chandelier in balance with the table, which means it should never be too small (most people make this error) or too large. Long, rectangular tables can even be lit by two or three smaller chandeliers.

The flickering glow of table candles is swell, but have you noticed how they never provide quite enough light? Try supplementing candles with electrified or real candle sconces on either side of a picture or mirror or over a buffet table.

Crystal and china bask in a glow of warmth from cabinet lights (easily

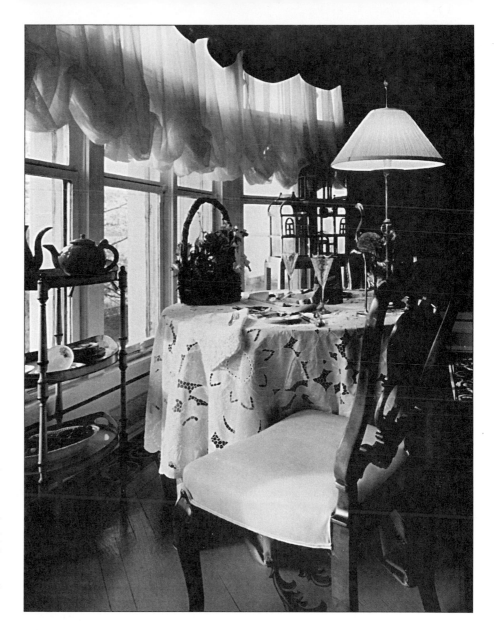

A tiered tea cart is a host's right hand. A crisp antique-lace cloth creates a spontaneous dining place. Billowing sheer balloon curtains add freshness.

Design by Ann Tarasoff at Mansions & Millionaires; photography by Oleg March.

installed by professionals); also consider installing lights in bookcases, hutches, and other niches where art is displayed.

EASY DINING

Once you settle the question of table and chairs, comfort won't be served until convenience is. Here are two hallmarks of easy dining without which you cannot do:

Unruffled service means a buffet surface—a place other than the table (usually a beautiful, adjunct piece of furniture) on which to rest platters, extra cutlery, dessert dishes. Any wall shelf mounted on two brackets can serve as a buffet. A tea cart, a rolling food-warmer stand, or even a French baker's rack also make beautiful buffet servers.

A room set aside just for dining is usually large enough to hold an eye-catching piece of storage furniture. Instead of the traditional breakfront, consider an antique armoire or even glassed-in bookshelves to hold cutlery, linens, and china.

STAGE-SET DINING

I wouldn't want to sleep in a stage-set bedroom or socialize in a stage-set living room, but a theatrical dining spot can be great fun. If you have a separate dining room, consider turning it into a a fantasy spot: Something charmingly different and elegant in decoration is a marvelous spur to sociability. The idea is to make mealtime a celebration of good food and company and how better to do this than with a little "theater"? If, for example, your home has an Eastern atmosphere, the dining room might reflect a Persian or Moroccan theme: tented fabric ceilings, fabric walls, and touches of Far Eastern imagination in art would make a wonderful place to feast and dream with friends.

A classic nineteenth-century French design umbrella might be finely accentuated with a dining room reminiscent of a turn-of-the-century French bistro: Two or three small circular tables instead of a grandly sized table, wall-mounted globe lights, and bentwood chairs can make dining an *experience*.

FINALLY, THE ART OF DINING

I love dining room art that is personal and passionate: your children's masterpieces, magnificently framed, a collection display, a vibrant watercolor of fruits or vegetables—dining room art is a happy adjunct to artful cuisine.

THE DUAL-PURPOSE DINING ROOM

If we're lucky enough to have a room set aside for dining, most of us do something else in that room as well. When we're not dining, we need to get more mileage from the same four walls. Perhaps we use part of it as a gathering room—a slightly different vista where dessert and before- or after-dinner drinks take on a new festivity—even if the same people are involved. It's fascinating to see how conversation freshens and fixed opinions change simply by slightly altering the view.

Perhaps we use part of the dining room as a library, media room, guest room, play or homework room, or even as a small office. Perhaps it's where our prized plants live. Perhaps it's where we show off our antique-book collection.

*D*ual-purpose dining:
Under the whitewashed
attic eaves, one may
nap, soak in a tub, or
entertain a lover at an
intimate dinner. Fresh,
antique lace "puddles"
over any round table to
create an "anywhere"
dining room.

Design by N. Gargiula and
M. M. Rinaldi; photography by
Bill Rothschild.

A dual-purpose hall-
dining area is anchored
by an overhead light.
When the table is not
set for dining, the vase
and fresh flowers are its
grace note.

Design by Carl D'Aquino
Interiors; photography by
Guy Lindsay.

An intimate dining spot can be anchored by art. A "puddling" tablecloth softens the architectural line of the contemporary chairs.

Design by M. (Group) Incorporated; photography by Carol Bates.

Often a dining room is also a music room, with a piano tucked into an opposite corner.

Whatever its dual purpose, the trick is to *set off* the dining area from the room's other reason for being. This is how to do it.

SET OFF WITH LIGHTING

A ceiling fixture anchors a table. It is a focal point delineating the center of a place. By hanging a wonderful chandelier off-center with the table directly beneath, one effectively divides the room. At the other end of the room, a smaller table surrounded by a small convertible couch and comfortable chairs now becomes a sitting area that can even double as a guest room.

In addition to ceiling fixtures, light *intensity* can also divide a room. The dual-purpose area, bathed in obscuring light (thanks to a dimmer), comes to life when the light is more pronounced and the dining area, in turn, gets "dimmed out."

A different *type* of lighting also separates the function of a room. The dining area may be served by a chandelier, but wall sconces, lamps, track lighting, or even a smaller chandelier to light the secondary portion of the room effectively change the mood as well as the purpose of a room.

SET OFF WITH SCREENS

A charming hand-painted screen is a perfect room divider. Screens can be constructed of glass bricks, mesh, beads . . . just about anything. Even a stark outline of a screen—say, a large rectangular steel frame—with nothing in the middle—effectively sets off a space.

SET OFF WITH FLOOR TREATMENTS

An area rug in definite contrast to the rest of a carpeted room distinguishes and sets off one area. Wooden inlays of intricate design or contrasting colors set into one end of a simple hardwood floor set off an area. Stenciled borders or patterns define areas.

SET OFF WITH FURNITURE

Bookcases, two club chairs, or a couch turned to face away from the dining table can make a room multipurpose.

SET OFF WITH A FOCAL POINT

An interesting focal point like a wonderful country-tiled fireplace, a glittering Baccarat chandelier, or a view of your pool also anchors a dining room area, keeps it separate, keeps it from floating into another part of the room being utilized for some other purpose. Make sure your dining table and chairs face or surround the focal point.

BUT WHAT DO WE DO WITH ALL THE EXTRA DINING CHAIRS?

Sometimes, in the dual-purpose dining room, the table must be disguised as a game or display table, and to carry off the disguise, you must get rid of the extra chairs. Many people choose folding dining room chairs for exactly this reason, but what is gained in utility with a folding chair is lost in comfort. A folding chair rarely hits the peak of quintessential comfort.

Try to choose real, good-to-sit-in chairs for dining, and if you have to make compromises, select smaller chairs.

Opt for "all of a piece" chairs that complement (in style or fabric) the furniture in the adjacent room. Then, when the need arises, you can easily disperse the chairs in the adjoining room or even place them against the wall, single file, without compromising the color or design of either room. When not in use, small chairs can even be hung on the dining room wall, as the Shakers did. If they look as if they belong there, they'll add to your general decorating scheme with artistic strokes of color.

The Anywhere-You-Find-It Dining Place

Let's face it: Real people eat all over their homes—in the media room, so as not to miss the Academy Awards, on the terrace when the air is fragrant and the trees are green, in a foyer where the telephone is and a long conversation *must* take place.

It's a good idea to keep these and other dining places in reasonable proximity to the kitchen, but generous trays and helping hands can always overcome problems.

Make these anywhere-you-find-them dining spaces the essence of social comfort to share with family and friends! For example:

Under the Stairs

A small, round pull-up table for two, four, or even six fits perfectly in a space that would be otherwise ignored or wasted. Here's the perfect corner

Dining can happen . . . under the stairs. Let's have breakfast or lunch!

Design by Rena Fortgang Associates, ASID; photography by Bill Rothschild.

*O*r *over the stairs . . .*
Design by Michael Love, ASID;
photography by Bill Rothschild.

for a companionable late-night supper with your mate, cocktails with a pal,
or even an intimate brunch with the next-door neighbors. Bowing to space
constraints, you may have to trade the club chair for the bentwood pull-up,
but pad the seat in charming fabric, upholster a feet-up-comfort bench in
coordinating fabric, provide important paintings and maybe even a grandfather clock to fill out and distinguish the area, and you have a cherished
and personal dining place.

IN A CORNER OF THE LIVING ROOM

And what if you have no extra space at all? You can still have a delightful dining place—right in your living room. Set off and anchor an area from
the rest of the room (just as you would in a multipurpose dining room) with
a rug, lighting, a visual focal point—or all three. Your outsized coffee table
(before you buy it, make sure it's the right height for seating comfort) is now
transformed into an elegant dining table. Your lush couch and coordinated

In a living-room corner . . . in front of a pillowed window seat, which provides half the seating. Pull-up living-room chairs complete the circle. Formal but relaxed ambience is the order of the day.

Design by Barbara Ostrom; photography by Bill Rothschild.

(not necessarily matching) side chairs provide the seating. After the meal, the chairs again become living room chairs, and the dining table metamorphoses back into the coffee table.

IN A MAKE-BELIEVE GARDEN

Gardens can be real or suggested. Terraces high above a city or garden rooms that never really see the sun are marvelous places to dine al fresco. Flowering plants, flowered fabrics, garden-lattice wallpaper, perhaps even a hanging swing to attend a flowery-clothed table can visually bring the outdoors inside. If you're lucky enough to have a real garden view outside your make-believe garden room, glass walls and carefully planned outdoor lighting will heighten the drama of the setting.

In a make-believe
garden . . . The dining
table—partly obscured
by the inviting
crocheted hammock—
and the feet-up wicker
furniture epitomize
Tranquil Country.

Design by Barbara Ostrom;
photography by Phillip H. Ennis.

ON A TERRACE

There's nothing so delicious as a dining place on a real porch or terrace, shaded from the sun but open to the sky. Wrought iron is a natural for terrace furniture, but don't make the mistake of choosing standard stiff, tiny wrought-iron chairs to match. Instead, upholster your airy furniture as you would a living room chair, using weather-impervious but sybaritically plush fabrics.

IN A HALL

Finally, one of the prettiest dining places I ever saw was in the entrance hallway of a tiny apartment. No dinner for twelve there, but never mind, we lingered for hours in the intimate coziness . . .

Media den: Fifty-three-inch rear projection television and a one hundred CD library for comfortable listening.

Design by Norman Michaeloff; photography by Phillip H. Ennis.

V HIGH-FUNCTION COMFORT

···

The house is a machine for living in.

—LE CORBUSIER

Even in the most traditionally decorated home, technology is all. The electronics, the appliances, the cutting-edge equipment we choose help us not only to function beautifully in our homes, but *keep* us home.

Suddenly, everything we need is right here—our workplaces, our working-out places, our cooking-in places, the sybaritic baths, and the media centers that cater to our senses. Suddenly the center of our universe is home—because it *works.* High technology, brought to one's fingertips, is comfort with its arms around function.

"The house is a machine for living in," said Le Corbusier, one of the most famous architects of the twentieth century.

To make the home a more efficient place of beauty was his goal—and ours: That's high-tech comfort.

We aim for bathrooms that are designed for optimum self-indulgence, storage and privacy; kitchens that are food- and people-friendly; home offices that do what the CEO's office does but in a private not a public space, and finally, home media rooms where the cutting edge of entertainment and personal relaxation are a paean to the good life. Saturday night may never be the same!

Practical, beautiful, high-tech rooms that are comfortable for all is the gift that living in the nineties makes possible.

THE BATHROOM: THE SECRET SPA

Not very long ago, the bathroom was considered merely a utilitarian space for cleansing the body of surface and interior wastes. Today, it has become a center for personal restoration, grooming, and relaxation; transcending pure utility, the bathroom can now be the place where body and soul reign together.

In fact, today's bathroom, combining the hedonistic and the functional, is a nineties version of the European spa, an approach to personal attention that has been around since before the ancient Romans. With the advent of shower massages, saunas, whirlpools, and aromatic personal-care products, formerly prosaic acts like bathing, shaving, and makeup application are elevated into rituals. Add a small bookshelf, space for music or story tapes, and you have no less than a secret spa with healthy self-focus as its *raison d'être*.

Everyone ought to think of her bath as a Secret Spa.

Create one!

COMFORT ZONE CHECKLIST: THE BATHROOM

ON FUNCTION

What do you *do* in the bathroom besides take care of your physical needs. Do you

apply cosmetics?

read?

listen to music?

talk on the telephone?

style your hair?

shave?

What are your special preferences—the techno-*musts* for your bathroom?

steambath

whirlpool

sauna

bath large enough for two

stall shower—no tub

tub—no shower

tub-shower combination

Are there people with special needs (elderly, injured, or very small) who will use the bathroom?

ON SPACE

How many people will use the bathroom? Just you, just you and your partner, or just you, your partner, and a dozen others?

Will you need to enlarge the bath physically? Visually?

ON TOILET FACILITIES

Do you want a bidet in addition to the toilet?

Do you need privacy for the toilet area—some way to set it off and out of view?

ON WATER

What kind of water pressure do you prefer in the sinks and shower—gentle, forceful, massaging action?

Do you find inconvenient the way the showerhead has been mounted on the wall?

ON STORAGE

Where will you keep sponges, shampoos, and moisturizers?

Where will you keep extra soaps, toilet paper, etc.?

Where will you keep cosmetics and medicines?

Where will you keep fresh towels?

Where will you keep dirty linens?

ON PSYCHIC COMFORTS

Do you like fresh greenery, artwork, extra mirrors, fragrances, or bibelots in your bath? Is there ample wall and surface space for display?

Do you need towel- or floor-warming devices?

Do you like extensive mirrored surfaces?

ON MAINTENANCE

Are you educated about surfaces that are durable, impervious to dampness, responsive to an easy mop, yet pretty to the eye and comforting to the touch?

About Plumbing

Surely it is possible to decorate on your own, but if you're planning to deal with plumbing, you need help. Whether you build from scratch or just intend to remodel an existing bathroom, work with a professional. Get an estimate of costs and the time involved from an experienced designer, architect, or contractor. Even major work can be surprisingly affordable if you have as an ally someone who knows what she's doing. On the other hand, attempting even the most modest plumbing creativity on your own can turn out to be a financial and emotional disaster.

Trends Toward Comfort

Here's the newest thinking about the comfortable bathroom.

Large master baths of the last decade celebrated togetherness to an exaggerated extent:

In were giant whirlpool baths where couples could steep together.

In was one vanity with his and her sinks.

In were toilet, bidet, storage areas lined up in an exposed, communal room.

What happened? Couples found that they rarely felt like soaking at the same time or jostling for space at the same vanity. We decided that of all the rooms in our home, the bathroom was the one place where we didn't want to act like grown-ups, didn't want to cooperate, compromise, or, worst of all, share. As we spent more time at home, we began to place more value on moments of privacy.

Thus, like many other rooms in the nineties home, the bathroom, which hasn't seen real change in a decade, also begins to sport little nooks and crannies—islands of coziness and insularity—within the larger room.

Further, as more and more of us of varying ages and physical abilities came home, reshaping of bathroom space and relocating of major elements seemed crucial.

Out goes the bathroom of the eighties.

In come new solutions geared to the nineties family that craves efficiency, convenience and most of all comfort.

Zone Your Bathroom

Enter zones or compartments.

Placing vanities, toilets, bidets, and whirlpools into alcoves or private, enclosed zones makes them seem more intimate, more user-friendly. We've discovered that a large, exposed bathing and toilet area combined with the

Zone your bathroom into private, user-friendly compartments. Here, the toilet area is hidden behind a door. The small bath is made grand by marble that sweeps up from the floor, around the tub, and up the wall. Mirrors seem to double the space.

Design by Bill Delsener; photography by Bill Rothschild.

ubiquitous bathroom tile and porcelain makes us feel exposed and vulnerable instead of comfortable and protected—especially when we're naked. The zoning concept rethinks available space and places the major bathroom equipment in protected and private recesses. It feels good.

Alcoves or zoning walls can be constructed in many ways. Here are three:

- "Pocket doors"—constructed to disappear by sliding into a wall—give the option of space-saving open or closed doors. Wood or translucent sandblasted glass make wonderful pocket doors.
- A half-wall constructed of glass bricks, a painted screen, or even a judiciously placed bookcase can create a private toilet alcove.
- Lattice or bamboo or bead screening or a fabric pull-down shade can create a private zone.

INDIVIDUALIZE

Separate but equal vanities and sinks are more efficient for storage and usage than the shared vanities of the seventies and eighties. And, although it sounds cozy, a shared shower more often makes for one shivering occupant while the other steams nicely under the water spray. Thus, individual space-saving showers and tubs, rather than the oversized variety, and individual vanities or pedestal sinks, rather than the shared version, are making a comeback.

DESIGN FOR REALITY

Although today you may plan your bathroom for two able-bodied young warriors, reality suggests otherwise. At different times in life, one of you may be pregnant, someone may be broken-legged, children may enter the picture, you may even, God forbid, grow old. Reality design is a lifetime design for high-tech comfort in your bathroom: It makes the bathroom more accommodating throughout life, to users of varying ages and abilities. It may include:

- faucets with preset temperatures to prevent scalding and single-lever faucets instead of individual hot and cold controls
- wider doorways to accommodate crutches or even wheelchairs
- doorless showers with extra-wide entrances
- adjustable-height wall-mounted showerheads or ceiling-mounted showerheads that require no adjustments for size
- handheld showers as an accessory
- shower seats or benches
- a minimum shower size of 36 x 42 inches instead of the 30 x 30-inch size that makes bending over difficult
- placing shower controls in a place where water temperature can be adjusted without having to dive right through a too hot or too cold spray
- nonskid surfaces in tubs and showers

The door handles, ramps, grab bars, safe floor surfaces, and other changes originally geared to help the permanently or temporarily handicapped can make life more comfortable for all of us.

THE CUTTING EDGE

If you're planning a new face for your bathroom, have a look at the cutting edge of high-tech comfort, now on the market.

TUBS

A chapter could be written just on new, more comfortable tubs alone. For example:

- extra-deep tubs
- tubs that accommodate two people

The cutting edge of baths often includes a place to sit in the shower/steam room. Painted tiles provide aesthetic harmony.

Design by Jarro Building Industries; photography by Carol Bates.

- Japanese soaking tubs to use after the soaping-up
- hot tubs
- soft tubs (designed from a "give" material that's remarkably easy on an achy body)
- molded contour tubs (some with seats)
- whirlpool massage tubs
- tubs that open from the side with a small door so you don't have to climb over the edge

SAUNAS AND STEAM BATHS

Other possibilities for your high-tech bathroom include a sauna, a steam bath, (you can convert a regular shower stall with a mechanism no larger than a bread box), and, as its manufacturer, Kohler, puts it, an *environment* enclosure with a choice of dry or wet heat, sun (lamp), or rain.

And don't forget the electronic gizmo that, when adjusted in the morning, draws your evening bath at precisely the proper time and at your favorite temperature.

TOILETS

Specialized toilets that are designed to fit into corners or to be suspended from the wall so that the floor beneath can be cleaned are on the market, as are soft toilet seats for all models.

A fluted, painted ceramic pedestal sink and profusely floral wallpaper are signals of a Fine Traditional Victorian era powder room.

Design by Alvin Schneider Design, Inc.; photography by Derrick-Love.

Sinuous stainless steel, wall-to-wall mirrors, and high-tech lights signal a Sleek Contemporary guest bath.

Design by R. Scott Bromley, Bromley Caldari Architects; photography by Jaime Adiles Arce.

SINKS

And sinks: Apart from a myriad of styles—from Victorian painted porcelain to contemporary hammered brass, steel, or chrome—sinks now come with comfort in mind: roomier ledges, spray attachments, and swing-away spouts, and for people in wheelchairs, special shallow-depth models.

WHAT ELSE AND WHY BOTHER?

Heated towel racks and heated floors, air purifiers and remote-control window openers are yours for the buying. Don't consider these technological advances as mere luxury; they are manna for taut, overexerted muscles and for insomnia. For example, steam and sauna aficionados claim to experience a "Zenlike" state, similar to a runner's high, and they emerge from their baths feeling comforted, more alive and healthier. And the soothing effect of a warmed towel or floor on a frigid night is unimaginable—until you've tried it. Decorating for comfort prolongs life.

HIGH-TECH STORAGE

If you're lucky enough to have a very large bathroom, consider moving a closet or dressing area that is now part of the bedroom into the bathroom. This tends to further zone the bathroom into his and her territories as well as to keep the sounds of bathing and dressing from the sleeping quarters.

Making any size bathroom efficient and comfortable means finding ever more space for grooming accessories. Even though cabinet space within your bathroom vanity should be custom-shelved to meet your needs, no one has ever yet had quite enough storage space. Consider:

- building niches directly into the shower-bath wall to hold bath supplies. If this is not feasible, caddies that loop over the showerhead or straddle the bath are readily available.
- using divider trays in your vanity drawers to sort all the small items.
- trying lazy Susans in vanity cabinets for storage. With deep cabinets it's always a challenge to retrieve one rear bottle without knocking over all the others.
- placing an old repainted corner cupboard, an étagère, or narrow cabinets set at right angles in a corner.
- buiding hair-dryer holders into the wall or placing them on the inside of vanity doors.
- using a whole wall of built-ins or a modular storage system especially designed for bathrooms. Look for wasted space. Check the walls above the toilet, tub, or the end of a vanity; check under the sink and toilet tank and install shelves, cupboards, racks, grids, and bins.
- installing bathrobe or towel hooks on backs of doors.
- prettifying the toilet ledge, no beauty in itself, with porcelain or straw baskets to hold grooming products.

- creating an ad hoc storage area under an old-fashioned pedestal sink by surrounding the sink with a pretty fabric skirt. Underneath place Rubbermaid instant shelves or use the area as a clothes hamper.
- buying a heated towel rack. A comfort touch is a warm towel. In the old days, hollow towel bars connected to the hot water system were the only way to go. Today, what was a luxury for the rich is now a simple, several-tiered, plug-in towel rack, easily attainable by mail order, not to mention in good hardware stores.
- replacing the original meager medicine cabinet that came with your bathroom. Commercial cabinets in every decorating style are readily available. Many come in all-in-one mirrored versions with extras such as built-in electrical outlets, fluorescent lights, or even heating units to prevent mirrors from steaming up. Another way to go is to build shelves and then screen them with slatted or roller blinds. And where is it written that you can't have two or even three medicine cabinets—if space allows?

Who says you can't put an Oriental rug in the bathroom?

Design by William Manley, ASID, for Kohler; photography by Hedrick Blessing.

- displaying neatly folded towels on wicker shelves on the bathroom wall. One client nailed colorful buckets to the back of the bathroom door and used them to hold rolled-up towels.
- finding unusual sources for storage fixtures for a tiny bathroom. Look for fixures designed for boats, trailers, and even laboratories. Layered foldaway shelves, cupboards, racks, and pull-out bins are to be found in stores that cater to special industries.
- storing small items in see-through zippered sweater bags; they are pliable and sometimes more useful than shelves.
- using your imagination and pressing into use antiques or found objects that were designed for other purposes. Ancient coal or log carriers, turn-of-the-century spittoons, apothecary stands, delicate old trunks, a garden or child's seat—almost anything with a surface can be used gorgeously for towels, cosmetics, or other bathroom items.

BATHROOMS DON'T HAVE TO FIT UNDER THE UMBRELLA

A classically contemporary bathroom, splendid with glass and steel fixtures, fits under any design umbrella. It is appropriate with a European Renaissance living room, a country charm living room, or even a graceful Oriental flavor living room. If, for example, your home is decorated under a Classic Americana design umbrella, of course your bath will look wonderful with wallpaper depicting Civil War battle scenes, wood cabinets, and a pewter flagon collection on a shelf—but you're also home free if you opt for glass and steel without even a nod to Americana. Why? A gleamingly high-tech bathroom has a global reach. It adapts to any design unmbrella.

THE GREENHOUSE EFFECT

The bathroom is a perfect place to add graceful plants that thrive in damp, warm atmospheres. Philodendrons, geraniums, spathiphyllums, and anthuriums do well in rooms without sun; begonias, coleus, and colored-leaf plants thrive in bathrooms filled with natural light and sun. Ferns love steam and damp!

THE KITCHEN

Welcome to the hearth, the heart, the hub of the home—the All-American great room. In the eighteenth century, the kitchen really bore the name "great room" because it was the place where everything happened. It was here that cooking, eating, craftsmaking, and discussion of family matters took place.

In today's great room, all these things still happen. The one addition?

Everything's charming in this old-fashioned great room. The original cast-iron stove, handhewn pine table, ladder-back chairs, wicker settee, and ceiling fanlight lend unruffled hospitality. Tranquil Country touches of antique children's toys and ruffled pillows are delicious. Design by Lee Napolitano, Allied Member ASID; photography by Bill Rothschild.

Electronics. Enter all the fabulous entertainment and food-preparation devices. It may have been called a great room in the old days as an allusion to its size, but today we know it's the great room because of its character and its possibilities.

One of its possibilities is as a gathering place. In the nineteenth century, the servants took over the premises, and those working in the kitchen were sequestered from the life of the home. Early in the twentieth century, when the servants walked out of the middle-class American kitchen, family and friends walked back in. They've never left. Why should they? The new great room is the place that nourishes us, the room to which we gravitate for coffee and gossip, the gathering spot. When we all come together again at the end of the day, working men and women, snack-hungry kids, and an extended family of colleagues and friends are pulled, as if by a magnet, to the control center of the home.

All this happens, that is, if the control center is comfortable.

A *rocker, center stage in the kitchen, is the heart of the hearth.*

Design by Teri Seidman Interiors; photography by Carol Bates.

I recently designed a kitchen with an adjacent breakfast nook surrounded by windows. We wondered what to do with the large, open space in the center of the kitchen. Should we put a work island there even though we had plentiful counter space? An extra kitchen table and four chairs? We decided on the island, but before we had a chance to begin construction and because the bedroom was being painted, my client took her bedroom rocker, the wonderful, much-loved chair where she'd read her childhood stories, then nursed her children, and put it temporarily in the center of the kitchen near the phone so she could sit while talking.

She rocked and she relaxed and she rocked some more. And when the bedroom paint dried, that rocker never made the trip back upstairs. My client found its presence in the kitchen so wonderful that it changed the way she thought about that room. Why *not* have the kitchen be a place of surpassing comfort as well as high-tech function?

We anchored the chair on a painted floor cloth just to the left of center kitchen, added a marvelous antique table to hold not only her cup of tea, telephone, and address book, but the fax machine and home computer, which kept her not only in touch with her office but in control of the budgeting, calorie counting, shopping lists, and recipes that are the real and natural work of the kitchen.

For some time, every day, she sat in that rocker and loved her kitchen, and when she wasn't occupying her tiny personal oasis, every other visitor to the kitchen vied for occupancy. The humming machines of this ultramodern great room—the microwave, the frost-free refrigerator, the computer, the cappuccino maker, and the pocket-sized television—constitute the modern-day hearth of this streamlined kitchen. The rocking chair, the quintessential emblem of comfort, remains its heart.

DO THE RIGHT THING

An architect or contractor must be involved in your planning if structural changes need to be made, plumbing or electricity relocated or added, or gas lines altered. There are new governmental guidelines to be followed that apply to private as well as public room designs: for example, wider doorways for easier wheelchair access. Your designer should be conversant with them.

SCOUT THE TERRAIN

Too many people design kitchens only for good looks and give short shrift to high-tech efficiency. The kitchen is the most complicated room in the house, and before you buy even a hot plate, you should educate yourself about ways to make the room work like a dream.

Start with designer show houses: Wonderful old mansions in almost every city are regularly being decorated by top designers. These events are advertised in local newspapers. Check out the kitchens in these homes—the surfaces, counter arrangements, appliances, and the newest ideas for storage facilities. Jog your own imagination!

Hit the kitchen displays in department stores to get new ideas for gadgets and storage.

COMFORT ZONE CHECKLIST: THE KITCHEN

ON FUNCTION

Are you a serious chef or do you only use the kitchen for snacks and fast meals?

Do you/family/friends eat in the kitchen?

Are you usually alone in the kitchen—or do people chat, hang out, work, watch TV as you work?

Do noncooking activities often go on? Do you enjoy listening to serious music, working on hobbies or business tasks in the kitchen? Do you fold laundry or oversee children's homework in the kitchen? Is there enough storage and space for all these activities?

Does your kitchen lend itself to the *kind* of cooking you most often do: for example, sit-down dinners, barbecues, cocktail parties, grab-what-you-feel-like meals?

ON THE WALL

Do you want to display any or all of the following: pans, trivets, utensils, hanging baskets for herbs, onions, potatoes, dried flowers, or a clock, bulletin board, cutting-breadboard, or other item?

OFF THE WALL

Do you want to display on countertops any or all of the following: canisters, vitamin jars, dish rack, wine racks, utensil holder, napkin holder, salt and pepper shakers, cutting boards, food timer, pet-food holders, other?

ON PRACTICALITY

Does the work height of your present kitchen counters or cabinets give you a daily backache? Are they reasonably comfortable to others who frequently use the kitchen?

Is everything you need easily reachable in closets, drawers, bins, or shelves—or do you need to rethink storage?

Have you decided on the appliances you really use—and are you realistic about discarding the ones that have just gathered dust in the last few months?

Are you left- or right-handed, and in the past, have your cabinets or appliances been uncomfortable to operate because this factor was ignored?

How high can you comfortably reach without a ladder?

Can you stand for long periods of time on the floor surface you've chosen? (Tile, for example, is beautiful but hard on the feet and knees.)

Have you been troubled with inadequate lighting in past kitchens?

ON THE DESIGN UMBRELLA

Is it retro charm or gleaming, stainless-steel style or a combination that appeals to your eye?

Will wallpaper, paint, tile, or paneling best suit your decorating scheme?

What kind of floors fit under your design umbrella? Will they be easy to maintain?

ON MAINTENANCE

Are you forever:
- mopping a floor?
- chasing after crumbs that disappear in cracks?
- dropping things behind appliances that are impossible to move?
- despairing over scuff marks caused by traffic or scraping chairs or stools?
- having difficulty sponging even modest spills?

The shelter magazines (*Metropolitan Home* or *House Beautiful*) feature special issues with emphasis on kitchens.

THE CORNELL COMFORT TRIANGLE

In the fifties, a Cornell University study came up with this revolutionary plan, called the "work triangle," as a design for comfort. It's a simple system of equipment placement. The idea behind it? Too many steps and too much energy are wasted traveling between work areas in an inefficient kitchen.

The classic trio—stove, sink, and refrigerator—is at the heart of the kitchen landscape. Everything else around it should enhance the design. To make the work area most comfortable, suggests the Cornell study, try to place the three primary appliances at equidistant points of a triangle, comfortably near each other. Then:

- At the triangle point where the refrigerator is located, make sure food-preparation surfaces and storage for frequently used utensils are close by.
- At the triangle point where the stove is located, pot and pan storage, insulated gloves, and surfaces on which to place hot pots should all be within hands' reach.
- At the triangle point where the sink or dishwasher is located, make sure there are adjacent storage and areas to place dirty and clean dishes, detergents, and dishtowels.

Kitchen Work Comfort Triangle: Each leg should be between 4 and 8 feet long. The total of the three legs should be 12 to 23 feet. A fourth or fifth cooking location or a second sink or microwave may be added for flexibility.

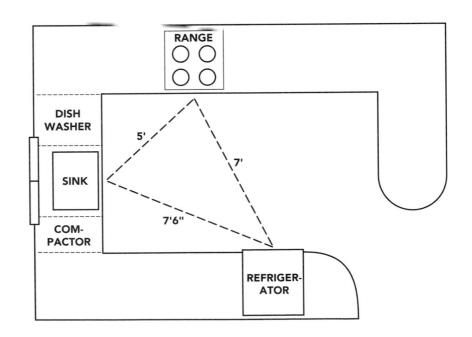

NOT JUST ANOTHER PRETTY FACE: IT WORKS

The same standards of efficiency that professional chefs use should apply to your kitchen as well. The height of the stove should permit the cook to peek into the tallest, bubbling pot (put the stove on blocks or a pedestal if necessary). The kitchen aisle should be wide enough for two people to work together, back to back—and, indeed, if you're planning major kitchen renovations, new laws make certain widths mandatory. Think about heights: Julia Child kept her toaster on top of the fridge, but if you do the same and you're not a six-foot-tall chef, you'll need to drag the ladder out every time you need the toaster—not terrific.

Unmatched, varying counter heights help create a comfort kitchen. Instead of standard overhead cabinets and plastic laminates, freestanding kitchen furniture—a pine hutch or oak or teak bookcases—can be used for food or dish storage. A farm table works as a center island around which people can gather, socialize, or help in the preparations.

For the highest level of comfort, plan the main countertop so the work surface is about 2 inches below your flexed elbow. Adjacent counter levels from 8 to 12 inches below the first could accommodate that toaster, the can opener, and food processor as well as provide some leverage to uncork wine. These lower levels are also children-friendly, providing a place for even the smallest to lend a hand. And consider varying *depths* of standard appliances: A very deep sink, for example, will more comfortably hold your largest pots and carving boards.

THE MARVELS

Which electronic marvels are essential to the comfortable functioning of your kitchen? Remember, you need a place to put each one.

coffeemaker	espresso/cappuccino maker
wall/surface telephone	knife sharpener
answering machine	coffee grinder
juice extractor	air conditioner
yogurt/pasta/ice cream maker	slow cooker
personal computer	ice crusher
toaster oven	toaster
electric wok	intercom
fax	electric fry pan
TV/radio	iron
ice cube maker	blender/food processor
microwave oven	Dustbuster
smoke/burglar alarm	timer
can opener	clock

WHAT ELSE?

THE BASICS

Determine what you want:
- electric or gas range
- one or two ovens (wall or freestanding)
- microwave oven (wonderfully convenient for the instant-baked-potato and soup-defrost jobs)
- gas-fired barbecue oven
- ice maker built into your frost-free refrigerator
- separate freezer
- `trash compactor or a garbage disposal

A note on sinks: Design-for-comfort kitchen sinks come in many designs like bottom-mounted, rimless versions flush with countertops for easy cleanup; they also come with options like retractable spray hoses, soap or hand lotion dispensers, instant hot or iced water dispensers, water purifiers for drinking water, and faucets with electronic readouts that indicate water temperature. Today, the basics include everything *and* the kitchen sink, so if you have a crazy idea for a timesaving comfort device but you've never seen it, ask around. Someone's probably invented your dream.

STORAGE: THE MAGIC WORD IS ORGANIZE

You've got to work with the space you have available. First, determine whether you like closed (get it all out of sight) or open (hang it, shelve it, stack it up) storage.

Then, organize as follows:

THE CABINET

Kitchen wall cabinets may be built to order by a cabinetmaker or bought as stock items and then assembled. The door styles on the cabinets should conform to your design umbrella; they range from Sleek Contemporary to woody country designs. The hardware you choose should complement the style; Lucite knobs, for example, are not so terrific on country wood doors.

Keep these tips in mind when dealing with cabinetry:
- It is possible to save money by replacing just the doors on existing cabinetry without touching the rest of the unit.
- If cups are hung in wall cabinets, make sure the hooks are adequate. There is nothing more annoying than a flimsy, not-up-to-the-job hook.
- Base cabinets (the top surface of these serve as counter space) should be looked at with an eye for comfort: By altering the size of the toeplate, your countertop can be higher or lower, depending on the most comfortable height for you.

A stunning, all-white contemporary kitchen has a clean-cut appeal. Ample preparation surfaces make for easy entertaining. Floor-to-ceiling and under-counter cabinets create superb storage.

Design by Joyce R. Wyman, C.K.D.; photography by Carol Bates.

☙ Besides base and wall cabinets, specialty cabinets tailored for specific needs (broom, vacuum cleaner, foldout ironing board, even hidden surfaces for extra dining space) can be custom-built or ready-made.

OTHER FOOD STORAGE

If you are lucky enough to have a separate room (a pantry or larder) for food storage, remember that shelves above eye level should graduate in depth so you can always reach to the back. Also keep in mind that swing-out racks with turning lazy Susan shelves are functional and marvelous.

BULKY STORAGE

Store bulky irons, baskets, large canisters, even the ironing board in lower, pull-out fittings: racks, bins, and drawers on runners to make your life easy.

ALTERNATIVES

Tall corner or wall units or creative furniture (like an old-fashioned armoire) can be fitted with doors, glide-out drawers of different depths, glide-out wine racks, silver storage compartments, trays for linen and cutlery, and cabinets specially made to accommodate cans, cereals, jams, flours, and other packaged goods.

LOOK AROUND FOR HIDDEN SPACE

Pull-out wire baskets snugged in under work areas can be used for fruit and vegetable storage. The space under the pet-food cabinet can be carved out to shelter the dog dish. Hideaway cabinets can be tucked into a pocket in the wall. Wire grids over windows or stoves can be rigged with hooks, shelves, or bins to organize odds and ends.

BUT WHAT DO I DO WITH THIS TEENY, TINY SPACE?

Shallow alcoves, corners, the undersides of cabinets or spare bits of wall can be pressed into service for bulletin boards or Peg-Boards, magnetic knife racks, towel racks, or a narrow cabinet just the width of single cans or bottles.

A WELL-LIT ROOM

There are three kinds of kitchen lighting. The latest lighting technology should be used in the kitchen. Poor kitchen light makes people cranky.

Task lights are lights directed to a specific place like a work surface or a reading area. Halogen spotlights are fine for this purpose.

General lighting is usually overhead fluorescent light that illuminates an entire area. It's possible to use a variety of fixtures, including chandeliers, hanging pendant lights, and track lights. Fluorescent lights are also fine for the inside of storage cabinets. General lighting, like good cabinetry, should be unobtrusive and effective: One should hardly even notice it.

Decorative lights are used for atmosphere. A chandelier over a table, for example, may not throw much bright light, but dimmed for ambience, it may set a mood for romance. A country kitchen will look fine with a hand-crafted iron chandelier.

THE FACE OF THE KITCHEN

The walls, floors, countertops, and general surfaces are the face of the kitchen. Like most beautiful faces, they are prettiest when they look and feel clean. If you are working under a design umbrella, the face of your kitchen ought to pick up on the materials, colors, and patterns that reiterate your design. A country kitchen, for example, is delicious with a hand-painted ceramic-tile face on the floor.

Vary the materials you use for contrast and excitement. A stainless-steel sink, a slate countertop, a quarry stone floor can all fit beautifully under a contemporary design umbrella.

Countertops: Slate and other good-looking stone surfaces are wonderful. Plastic laminates are less expensive and come in many colors and prints—even simulated natural materials like wood, butcher block, marble, and granite. While white is a traditionally popular countertop color, a pure black laminate is a newly popular option because, like polished stone, it reflects light beautifully. Ceramic tile, especially the hand-painted variety, is beautiful, and smooth-surfaced, machine-made tiles are even easier to maintain than uneven handmade tiles. Wood, stone, stainless steel, and raw concrete (which has been poured and sealed) are other options.

Walls: Monochromatic paint, a painted scene, wallpaper, wood paneling, or ceramic wall tile can cover the walls or serve merely as backsplashes.

Granite and wood countertops, floors, and walls echo the natural beach textures and colors in this oceanside great room.

Design by John Buscarello; photography by Keith Scott Morton.

Floors: Quarrystone, glazed or ceramic tile, vinyl, cork, linoleum, brick, slate, marble, or hardwood—the possibilities are endless. Remember that natural material that "gives" is comfortable and resilient underfoot. Wood, for instance, is a good choice if you need to stand for long periods of time in your kitchen.

A MORE COMFORTABLE TODAY

Finally, like my client with the rocking chair, visualize your kitchen as a resting place for sore limbs and sore spirit. Who says a chaise or a club chair doesn't belong in the kitchen? Who says banquettes under kitchen windows can't be lined with the plushest, most delicious pillows for reading and dreaming? Who says the kitchen can't be the cozy hearth every family member craves?

No one.

Think country: A sunny window seat in a country kitchen is a fine place to think about what to serve for lunch. Wall-hung shallow shelves display food fixins. Design by Shelley Azapian; photography by Bill Rothschild.

A MORE COMFORTABLE TOMORROW

There are a number of trends for "reality" or what has also been called *universal design* for the high-tech kitchen, just as there are for cutting-edge bathrooms.

- The kitchen should be accessible to elderly, youthful, or injured family members. Light switches, for example, should be set 40 inches from the floor (instead of the standard 48 inches) so they are within the reach of a small child or wheelchair occupant.
- Wing handles at the sink are shaped so they can be moved with a wrist (for arthritic fingers).
- Knobs on drawers and cabinets should be substantial, oversized, and easy to grip.

THE HOME OFFICE

In 1990 a prophetic AT&T advertisement appeared in national publications. The ad showed a man, his dog, and mankind's new best friend—the word processor—all perched on a homey redwood deck overlooking a verdantly green forest. With only junipers as far as the eye could see, the man looked, at once, perfectly free, perfectly comfortable, and perfectly plugged in to the world. For many consumers, the ad offered a glimpse of professional and personal lives in idyllic and peaceful balance.

An estimated thirty-nine million Americans go downstairs instead of downtown; that is, they work at home. While most of these people want their home workplace very high-function, they also want it to reflect the comforts of home.

The architect Christopher Alexander put it best when he said that today's office was "more childlike, more rooted in human feelings and more comfortable as environment; you want to be there in the same sense that you want to curl up in a corner with a pillow on a Saturday afternoon."

This new view of the workplace is changing the look of the corporate office as well; even there, hard-nosed CEOs are going for the "homey" office or, as *The New York Times* puts it, the "domesticated" office. In tall glass and steel office buildings, long conference tables with straight-backed chairs are giving way to coffee tables and couches; corporate grays and blues are yielding to warmer, more "residential" yellows; disparate patterns and nubby, warm textures are being seen in fabrics and carpets; in some eclectic cases, the furniture may not even match.

It's nothing less than decorating for comfort, and the home office started the trend.

The home office's beauty is that it's home. Art and beloved treasures dot the room. An antique urn is used for charts, and go-anywhere tables are pressed into service for note taking or snacks.

Courtesy of Essex Wallcoverings.

There's no place like home for a comfortable workplace: Whether you put in many or few hours, you deserve a spot that's all your own. Carving out work space may range from the luxurious (enclosing an attic or bumping out a house addition) to the modest (partitioning off a bit of privacy in a corner of a living room, kitchen, or bedroom) but whichever way you go, sleek new furnishings and state-of-the-art equipment should gladden your eye and comfort your body—even as they enhance your productivity.

Caveat: The one thing that's true of all home offices is that they must be separated from personal living space by a door, a screen, or another divider that says to one and all: *Do Not Disturb: I'm working and want to be left alone.* It also helps to be able to close the door on the office when work is done and leave—both practically and emotionally.

People who work at home are often asked, "But how do you discipline yourself to avoid distractions at home?" You do it by keeping the office totally separate from the incursions of kids, friends, and other incompatible domestic activity.

COMFORT ZONE CHECKLIST: THE HOME OFFICE

ON OFFICE FURNITURE

Will you be using the office for long periods every day, or just to do catch-up homework?

Will you have clients or visitors come to the office— or is it strictly seating for one?

Do you have a bad back? Do you like to stretch out periodically on a couch for relief?

What will your equipment live *on* (tables, desks, shelves)?

Do you need a reasonable or an unreasonable amount of work space on which to spread out projects and papers?

WHAT AMOUNT OF TIME DO YOU SPEND:

talking to one or more visitors?

dictating to a machine?

typing or writing longhand?

reading memos, magazines, statements?

drawing or sketching?

eating, drinking, catnapping (yes, you'll do all of them in your home office)?

talking on the telephone?

WHAT AMOUNT OF TIME DO YOU SPEND:

sitting upright?

slouching?

standing?

pacing about?

lying down?

ON OFFICE LIGHTING; ASK YOURSELF:

How can you best take advantage of the natural daylight that enters the space?

Are there areas shadowed by things like beams and overhangs? How will you work around them?

Will you have enough room and outlets for task lights (must be at least three times brighter that the overall ambient lighting),

ON EQUIPMENT

What follows is a list of the most important equipment you may need for your home office. The marketplace offers a dizzying array of products, too extensive to cover here adequately, so check the Resource Guide for more complete sources.

First, check off the essentials from the comprehensive list below just to get a practical idea of the space needed to house it all.

computer/word processor and printer

answering machine

fax machine

books (dictionary, thesaurus, maps, research and reference materials, phone)

telephones

copier

tape recorder

typewriter

tape-transcription machine

VCR

Rolodex

file cabinets

film projector

wastebaskets (large!)

paper shredder

clock

calculator

calendar

magazine file

desk equipment (staplers, tape holders, pencil-, pen-, paper clip holders, stationery, document tray)

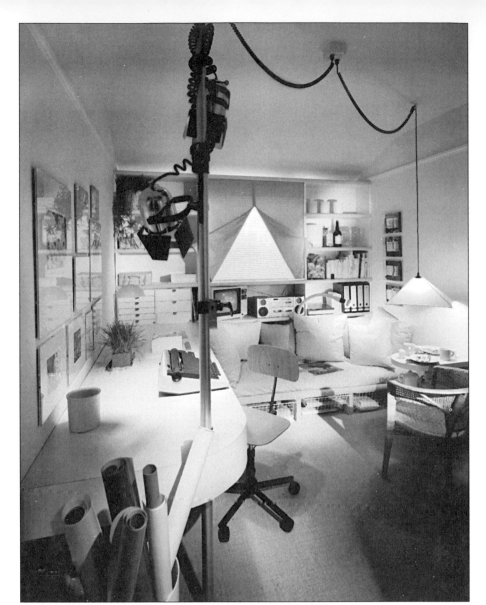

Ergonomic chairs give proper body alignment. The lengthy work surface allows freedom to spread out, and the built-in couch has easy wire-basket storage underneath. Niches, drawers, boxes provide extra storage.

Courtesy of Levilor; photography by Bill Rothschild.

Now, Have a Seat. No—Not That One, It's Mine!

Ludwig Mies van der Rohe, the Bauhaus architect, once said it was easier to design a skyscraper than a good chair. It's true.

Ergonomists, specialists in the study of how to adapt machines to people, point to poorly positioned keyboards, poorly lit computer screens, and deadline pressure as reasons for painful injuries to shoulders, arms, hands, and backs in the office. In your home office, all of these causes are possible—but if you hurt, it's most probable that you've got the wrong chair.

Besides causing aches and pains, too-high chairs can put pressure on the backs of thighs, trapping the blood in the lower legs and measurably increasing the size of the calves. Too low seats put the body at an angle that causes pressure on abdominal organs.

A good chair for the home office is an adjustable, ergonomic chair with moving parts that give proper body alignment whatever the adjustment. It should allow for a whole range of squirming about rather than just one seating posture. Ergonomically sound chairs are usually more expensive because more moving parts means more complicated production—but go for one for your desk at least! We need furniture that is gentle with us.

A good chair…

Should have mechanisms that adjust the height, tilt the backrest, and provide lower-back support. The best chairs also allow you to vary the tension of the chairback.

Although traditional typing chairs are usually armless, adjustable arm supports can reduce fatigue.

The chair's seat edges should be rounded.

Most experts think the base should be star-shaped with at least five spokes.

A good chair may be made even better by a small comfortable footstool. There's nothing like putting your feet up while working.

Finally, there are those who swear by those oddly shaped "back chairs" which have you half-squatting, half-kneeling at the desk (the best ones swivel or move on casters and are made in Scandinavia or England).

See the Resource Guide for the names of companies that design comfortable office chairs.

CAN A COUCH LIVE HAPPILY IN A HOME OFFICE?

A small couch is wonderfully appealing to visitors to your private domain as well as a perfect touch for the home-working sybarite who needs to dream, meditate, or just stretch out with a frozen yogurt in between deadlines. And don't ignore the classic easy chair (with ottoman), which provides a softer environment all by itself when the workload becomes unbearable.

CALL THIS A DESK?

Does it hold your typewriter-word processor, supplies, research materials? Do your legs fit under it comfortably both when you sit up straight to work and when you lean back to read? Do you have easy access to it and can you move your chair around comfortably without banging your shins every time you reach or stretch? Then it's a desk even if it looks like a…

- circle of textured black glass on a base
- slab of sea-green marble on a base
- painted door atop two file cabinets
- traditional rosewood-with-drawers desk

Call this a desk? Yes. It's spacious, multifunctional.

Design by Celia Vogel and Mario Mulea at Mansions & Millionaires; photography by Oleg March.

Also convertible.

The out-of-office desk can be a beauty! Ample work surface, nearby alternative storage (an antique box on a handy ottoman), and a distinctively stylish (but comfortable) chair invite efficiency.

Design by Karen Houghton Interiors; photography by Bill Rothschild.

Be imaginative and consider a small dining-room table for a desk. If, as a child, you've ever done homework on one, you know why; it's familiar, comfortable, it evokes nurturing and safety, and it's big enough to spread work out on. It's fascinating to note how the focus of the room becomes the wonderful dining table/desk and not your plastic word processor. The extra benefit, of course, is that the desk serves as a dining table when needed.

If you have a Sleek Contemporary design umbrella, consider a richly textured stone or marble dining table.

If you have a Fine Traditional design umbrella, consider an antique Louis XIV table or even an old English library table (with old-fashioned shaded lamps at each end to evoke that warming, hushed European library feel).

If you have a Tranquil Country design umbrella, how about a distressed-wood butcher-block dining table desk?

THE OUT-OF-THE-OFFICE DESK

Whether you have a home office or not, you may want a desk in another room as well, a different kind of desk.

Although these desks may also be used for heavy-duty work, their decorative appearance is as important as their function, and they should take on the character of the room in which they live.

A desk in the living room, for example, should have a roll top or other cover to conceal papers when company comes. It could be an exquisite burl walnut William and Mary masterpiece for a Fine Traditional living room, a hand-painted charmer for a Tranquil Country decor, or a tall secretaire that comes in many styles. Incidentally, secretaires, which are desks combined with drawers and shelves, provide additional storage space, and because furniture of varying heights lends visual interest to any room, they are useful points of attention.

A bedroom desk should be intimate as well as functional to reflect the voluptuous nature of the room. Instead of the hard-edge, high-tech office version, the bedroom writing table is a surface for the flowers you love and the bibelots that define you as well as the place to pen your notes, your poems, even your bills. It may even serve as a night table if placed on one side of the bed.

My own bedroom desk has a drop leaf that closes, for serenity's sake: Great psychic comfort derives from not having to look at the paper clutter.

AT LAST—A WINDOWED OFFICE!

Even if your home workplace finally affords the window office that was unavailable in the corporate world, make sure that the glare from the outdoors doesn't make your computer terminal hard on the eyes. A computer screen is basically a mirror and reflects even the smallest glare on the screen.

Don't put your desk directly in front of or behind a window that's in line with direct sunlight. If you have no choice, consider a terminal hood or an antireflection screen to shield you from glare.

LIGHTEN UP

Only a gentle light is comfortable, so use task lighting—like a high-tech Italian Tizio desk lamp with a bendable arm (or even a traditional "banker's" desk lamp with a green shade), a downlight, or a ceiling spot for your work. Go for a 100-watt halogen for the highest level of task lighting. Avoid center ceiling lights. Most offices are overlit anyway. Certainly avoid traditional, bright, glare-causing fluorescent lights that may also give off an annoying buzz in the close quarters of a home office. If you use your office for after-business-hours entertaining, use accent lighting on personal collections or artwork.

STORAGE

"You clinking, clanking, clattering collection of caliginous junk!"
—THE WIZARD OF OZ TO THE TIN MAN

Even if it doesn't clink and clank, you've got to stow it. Great storage is a real priority in the home office, especially if the room is a multipurpose

Built-in storage makes life easy.
Design by David Walker; photography by Peter Vitale.

Built-in storage can be softened with shirred curtains on concealing doors.
Design by Stephanie Stokes, Inc.; photography by Walter Smalling.

room. Storage comes in nice style touches that would probably be inappropriate in a more corporate setting. Try:

- turn-of-the-century log carriers
- dental cabinets
- porcelain canisters and other "holders"—great homes for paper clips, reams of paper, and other office supplies.

Behind closed doors (as in walk-in closets), a multitude of sins can be stashed on levels of wire shelving, in file cabinets, and annexed to bulletin boards.

An entire wall of the closet or office can be paneled with painted or natural sheet cork thick enough to take long pushpins as well as thumbtacks.

Finally, bookcases—high-tech steel and glass or heavy polished wood—can store on their shelves, not only books but also pretty boxes filled with office stuff. An office lined with beautiful bookshelves is wonderful, and some of those shelves can be used for the personal treasures and collections that make an office a home.

PHONES

A separate telephone is to a home office what a sink is to a bathroom—it defines the place. For real comfort, consider a model that includes a speaker or a comfortable headset so that you can free your hands and move beyond the limits of a phone cord.

FLAIR

Flair follows function. First, your office must work. Then, it should be rich with personal flair. Your design umbrella can be carried out here as well as in the living room, with carpeting, wall textures, and objets d'art all of a design piece. Remember that your flair will most effectively evolve into high style if you try for simple effects. There are a lot of things going on in a home office, and these various work functions shouldn't have to compete with elaborate tassels and twirls. However, feel freer here than, say, the dining room to stretch the 80/20 rule (see page 11) in the design umbrella concept. Even if your style is Fine Traditional and your weathered typewriter Hemingwayesque, a sleek chrome desk lamp will not clash with the overall effect.

We Cannot Live by Computers and Copy Machines Alone

Just as important in the high-tech office as the latest in ergonomically designed furniture or fax machines, are the small touches that reassure a working ego. You still have to do the work, but a comfortable home office helps to insulate you against work-related stress. Sensory cues like a goldfish swimming in a tiny tank, a bonsai tree, or rocks from the sea not only bring the outside in but provide block-breaking relaxation.

One writer keeps framed copies of his best work on the wall to remind himself that he's done it before and he can do it again.

A freelance accountant keeps toy pandas on his desk and a collection of refined erotica on his wall—objects that might be taboo in a stuffy corporate environment.

A graphic artist has decorated her windowless office with poster-sized photographs of her favorite places in Europe; they remind her that there's a world out there.

Yet another home worker swears by the cheery purr of her office cappuccino maker and a recorded mantra with which she starts each work session.

To each his own. We cannot live by copiers alone.

THE MEDIA ROOM

There's nothing new about media rooms. People have always enjoyed gathering at home for communal entertainment in multipurpose rooms. In the old days, they gathered in the great hall of the castle to witness a theatrical presentation, listen to someone play a viola da gamba, gossip, play cards, drink tea, or flirt. This place where friends and family came together to seek entertainment collectively was always the liveliest room of the castle.

Very litle has changed today except that the lively room is also the electronic heart of a home, with rustic stages and ornate tapestries giving way to a gaggle of lights, dials, toggle switches, and slide controls that can look more like the control panel of the starship *Enterprise* than a room in one's home. Still, friends and family continue to play, be entertained, gossip, and flirt in this fun, fully equipped common room as we all turn our backs on the strobe-lit discos, high-priced restaurants, and frenzied single-bars of past decades. As baby boomers ease into middle age, three times as many people say they'd rather watch a movie at home than go out to see one.

Home media rooms have even become a status symbol; this is also nothing new, since glitzy Hollywood types have considered a personal screening room to be a status symbol since the twenties. Home media rooms, however, complete with state-of-the-art audio-video systems, are pure nineties. Remember the theatrical thrill we felt when we first heard the spaceship roar overhead in *Star Wars* and *Close Encounters*? Relatively inexpensive home-audio components can create the same effect.

But take the most sophisticated media equipment ever devised, put it in a pretty room—and if you don't feel comfortable, you won't want to stay.

The architect Christopher Alexander gave this definition of comfort:

Imagine yourself on a winter afternoon, with a pot of tea, a book, a reading light, and two or three huge pillows to lean back against. Not in some way which you can show to other people, and say how much you like it. I mean so that you really *like it for* yourself. *You put the tea where you can reach it but in a place where you can't possibly knock it over. You pull the light down, to shine on the book, but not too brightly, and so that you can't see the naked bulb. You put the cushions behind you, and place them carefully, one by one, just where you want them, to support your back, your neck, your arm; so that you are supported just comfortably, just as you want to sip your tea, and read and dream.*

Add to Alexander's last words "or watch a movie, listen to a song, record a conversation, catch a favorite television show or just talk…," and you have the quintessential description of the comfortable home media room.

The electronic hearth: A rear projector defines home theater—minus the waiting in line.

Design by Evan Galen, Inc.; photography by Mary Nichols.

A *Sleek Contemporary setting: Built-ins, which include a bar, stereo-system storage, and the ubiquitous television, take center stage in the home media room.* Design by Jennie Curland Interiors; photography by Bill Rothschild.

COMFORT ZONE CHECKLIST: THE MEDIA ROOM

Is the media room used primarily for individuals, family togetherness, or family *and* friends?

How much seating do you need?

How much table surface?

How much storage? Do you want your equipment to be hidden away when not in use—or do you want to accent the shapes and colors of the components themselves as part of the room design?

Will you stay within a design umbrella? (You don't have to!)

Are you totally knowledgeable about the latest in equipment and ease-of-function accessories? Can you find a mentor to shepherd you through the literature and the stores?

WHAT GOES IN THE ROOM?

Anything that gives you pleasure, ranging from backgammon tables to music stands, from Scrabble sets to puzzles. Since the media room is the nineties answer to the family den, all your hobbies (watching the moon through a telescope, stamp collecting, pool playing) probably take place here too, in a room that eases the functioning of such activities. But most of all, electronics go in this room.

ELECTRONIC PLEASURES

Here are some possibilities for your media room. They all are based on the television components and the sound systems you choose. Naturally, before you buy, educate yourself on the best brands by talking with experts and reading magazines like *Consumer Reports.*

THE TELEVISION SET

It's still the basic component of home entertainment. However, the television set's newest functions seem endless. Beside the regular programming that we know and love/hate, the television is used for:

- VCRs (videocassette recorders), which permit us to watch leased movies or recapture broadcasts to be played on our own time schedules
- videodisc players, which increase program choices and add a new dimension through stereo sound.
- interactive video-games
- home computers and systems that permit linking with computers outside the home

And don't forget the remote control, which offers the comfort of channel-surfing from wherever you are in the room.

TRUE HOME THEATER

Home movies can be spectacular! Doing it right means a large-screen television set linked to a high-quality sound system with "surround-sound," which makes you feel *plunk* in the center of the action on the screen. Here's what you need:

- *Screen:* Ideally, you should use a ceiling-mounted projector that casts a wall-sized image. If you already have a large TV set with a screen measuring 27 inches or more, you can skip this expensive item, which can cost from $4,000 to $6,000, suggested price list.
- *Combination laser disc/CD player:* Movies on laser discs have sharper images and truer colors than those on videotape. With a player that plays both videodiscs and compact discs, your home theater can work for exquisite music listening as well as for watching

TV and videos. They cost between $550 and $800, suggested list price.

- *An audio-video receiver:* In addition to performing musical functions like a regular stereo receiver, the audio-video receiver coordinates the movement of the "surround-sound" with the on-screen action. They run from $450 to over $1,000, suggested list price.

- *Speakers:* The excitement of home theater comes from three-dimensional sound and the realism one feels at the local movie theater. You need five speakers to achieve this—left, right, and center front, plus two behind the listener. Together they range from $1,200 to $2,000, suggested list price.

    TIP: The inexpensive way to home-theater comfort? Celestion Systems in Holliston, Mass., has come up with a compact package that sells for well under $1,000 complete.

- *Comfort Options:* Generally, sound systems today have produced the most sophisticated audio components even if you're not committed to an entire home-theater setup. Depending on room size and shape, myriad sound-system options are available. Particularly interesting are new audio accessories that, because of the increased use of microprocessors, provide the highest level of convenience and ease of use: Touch one button—and you can electronically and automatically fine-tune radio stations. Preset favorite stations so that at a touch of another button, your most loved music instantly surrounds you. Program your tapes or records so you can listen to them in any sequence you wish. Remote control your turntable, tuner, amplifier. Shape the tone of your music with an equalizer. The options are endless.

WHERE DO I PUT ALL THOSE ELECTRONICS?

You are not the first person who's faced the problem of where to put the VCR and the TV, not to mention the computer, compact-disc player, and stereo components.

What a surprise—savvy manufacturers have designed beautiful, cable-accommodating pieces to hold everything in exquisitely crafted armoires, modular units, or desks that somehow coordinate with the finest sofas. Or, depending on your design umbrella, choose *not* to house the electronics at all but keep them marvelously visible with their bold looks—those matte-black stunners, those candy-colored fantasies!

If you choose housing for your electronics, consider the following:

- Swivels and pull-out shelves can be installed in armoires so that television sets can be turned to face any corner.
- Components can all be flush-mounted in the wall or placed in custom-made cabinets.

High-tech equipment fits beautifully under any design umbrella. Here, wicker and white dominate in a seaside media room. Note the unobtrusive media tower on the right. Design by Eleanor Leonard Associates; photography by Phillip Ennis.

- A television can be submerged in a hidden cavity of a center-room bar; when required, the television rises electronically at the touch of a button.
- Media systems can be sunk into room columns, becoming one with the architecture.
- Projectors can be concealed in coffee tables; wall-mounted tape-storage cabinets can be lacquered or mirrored; and flush doors can conceal any equipment at all.

THE SOUND AND LIGHT SHOW

Do you want to sit or recline (or both) in your media room? Where do you want to keep the remote controls, magnetic tapes, laser and floppy discs? What surfaces will you need for snacking or casual dining?

Sound: Plan your home media room for the best acoustics and consider how much the furniture, carpet, draperies, and other objects will obscure the sound. Walls containing layers of fiberglass or polyurethane soundproofing can be installed to encourage pure sound. Ask experts to advise on the best places to put the speakers.

Light: Apart from decorative lighting, which may come into play when the equipment is not being used, the principles of lighting while you watch the screen are basic and simple:

- A totally dark room doesn't lend itself to the best viewing.
- Never allow a light from another source to shine on the screen.
- Watch for obstructions blocking the screen from the audience.
- The best light source is from behind the viewer's head and aimed away from the screen.

Cozy comfort: A secluded corner provides an elegant nest of comforts. Note the privacy-making drapes, nurturing throw, deep pillows, surface for a book or cup of tea, the sinuous lines of the reclining chaise. I could hide here forever.

Design by Karen Houghton Interiors; photography by Bill Rothschild.

VI

COZY COMFORT

....

This is the true nature of home—
it is the place of peace; the shelter.

—JOHN RUSKIN

Home is where we go to feel cozy.

Comfort is complicated: The word is rich with different layers of meaning. Depending on who is defining it, comfort is convenience, body ease, psychological well-being, privacy—all of these things.

There isn't a person in the world to whom pure comfort doesn't *first* mean cozy. The Germans call it *gemütlich,* the Spanish call it *simpático,* we call it warm, peaceful, snug as a bug in a rug. We call it cozy comfort.

It was at the end of the eighteenth century in Britain that the drawing room was invented, and it was in the drawing room that the idea of cozy, which was to filter down to America, was born. Here, comfortable and easygoing furniture placement first crowded out the stiff-backed appointments of traditional English decor.

Tables and chairs no longer were placed against the wall but came to rest companionably in the center of the room. Sofas were pulled away from the perimeter of the room and placed at right angles to walls. Low tables (the first "coffee tables") were judiciously placed in front of sofas. Furniture groupings flanked fireplaces to make cozy corners.

The novelist Jane Austen wrote about one of her character's rooms as being a "nest of comforts."

And it is just that—the concept of *nest,* of a snug, padded, and peaceful shelter, that particularly evokes the sense of coziness we strive for—whether we live in a small, compact apartment or a grand and elegant home.

THE ESSENCE OF COZY

The intrinsic quality of cozy is smallness—or a sense of smallness. But even a cavernous space can be made to feel psychologically snug and warm when it's decorated with intimacy in mind.

NICHES, NOOKS, AND CRANNIES

Niches, nooks, and crannies are the coziest places in our home. They're secluded spots, usually miniature spaces for all seasons and all reasons; they envelop us for romance, privacy, or congeniality.

They have three requirements:
* They must be comfortable.
* They must be easy on the eye (there ought to be something beguiling to look at like an entrancing painting or a roaring fireplace).
* They must be near a surface on which to put a drink, a cup, a book, a pattern, a poem.

Three Red Flags: What's Not a Cozy Niche, Nook or Cranny?
* ramrod-straight seating with no footrests or room to curl up
* any place that's too dark or too light
* any place in the center of a traffic pattern

COMFORT ZONE CHECKLIST: THE COZY SPACE

NICHES, NOOKS, AND CRANNIES COZY

Have you scouted out your home for logical places to put a window seat, a tiny table and two chairs, a lush armchair and ottoman, or other groupings that invite intimacy? How about:
that calm corner in the kitchen for an intimate breakfast nook?
those few unused feet under the steps for a cocktail retreat?
that beckoning alcove in your attic or basement for a good read?
that warm circle in front of the fireplace for a good dream?
If you have no ready-made corner, have you thought about creating a niche just big enough for one, or two, maybe three?

COMMON ROOM COZY

Is there a relaxing room for the entire family to gather together? Is it geared and fitted out for every age group within the family?
Is there adjacent storage for the accoutrements of all the activities going on in the room?
Is the room easy-care, well lit for specific activities, and as soundproof as possible?

CHILDREN COZY

Are their rooms customized for them? For example, have they had input into decoration?
can they reach what they need to reach?
will their rooms grow with them?
is there adequate storage space?
is there child-size, child-friendly furniture?

COMPACT COZY

Is this your problem? You have a very small apartment or house. The good news for compact cozy is that small is intimate. The challenge is making the most of what you have so it feels comfortable and looks charming, not crowded.

AIRY COZY

Do you have an indoor or outdoor balcony/patio/terrace?
Do you feel intimate there—not vulnerable in wide, open, impersonal space?
Is it a hodgepodge of leftover, unappealing furniture? Would you like to learn how to accessorize this indoor-outdoor "room" for ultimate coziness?

Window-seat cranny. Design by Leslie Harris Interior Design; photography by Tina Street-Porter.

THE PERFECT SPOTS FOR NICHES, NOOKS, AND CRANNIES

A WINDOW SEAT

A long, sun-drenched, moon-lit pillowed platform under a window invites loungers, chatters, readers, nappers. Recessed lights or a glowing lamp provides the atmosphere when the sun goes down. Cozy and snug in the cut-out space under the window, the dreamer's room and view extend to the world outside, without her necessarily feeling part of that larger world.

Cozy window seats go anywhere—even in a more formal room. Here, an upholstered window niche is also a retreat. It affords an invisible sense of privacy even in the center of a social hub. The window on the world and art on the wall provide visual interest.

Wonderful art on a slant wall in a charming garret can make the coziest hideaway! A place to sleep, read, or entertain in calm spirit.   Design by Richard Mervis Designs, Inc..; photography by Michael Rogol.

A SITTING ROOM

Snug retreats in garrets or basement hideaways are places to read, share coffee, or stretch out together on an oversized divan. Standing screens can give a "view" even in a viewless corner; they also can make a large space more intimate by enveloping the nearby furniture.

A FIRESIDE CHAT

Anchored to a hearth, a sheltering nook near a fireplace provides psychological as well as real warmth. If there are two chairs, each should have its own reading light, its own soft pillow, its own convenient surface on which to place things—plus a shared footstool for camaraderie.

Classic comfort within a fireside nook. Downy pull-up chairs and a shared footstool are perfect for an intimate chat.

Design by Mark A. Polo for M. A. Inc.; Fort Lee, NJ; photography by Bill Rothschild.

JUST A CORNER

Every home has one—just waiting to be transformed into a cozy nook. The lushest of club chairs, the plushest of pillows under the most golden light make a tiny, perfect island.

JUST A WALL

That wall you don't know what to do with—in the dining room, an upstairs hall, a home office, or an entryway—can serve as backdrop to a "let's sit side by side" conversation nook. You'll need a surface on which to rest your tea, a footstool, and a view.

UNDER THE STAIRS

This may be the most intimate cranny of all. What a sheltering feeling to be roofed by a staircase and snuggled into an alcove. Don't waste this darling little patch of space.

Just a corner for curling up. Design by Teri Seidman Interiors; photography by Bill Rothschild.

THE COMMON ROOM: FOR CHILDREN OF ALL AGES

It used to be known as the family room or the den, but whatever you call it, it's the place that draws children of all ages together, and that includes adults. It won't draw if it's not cozy. Cozy is its raison d'être.

The common room is used for a variety of functions at different times. Sometimes family will gather to play together. Sometimes family will gather but play at individual pursuits. Two children may play Nintendo while another may wish to do a puzzle and Mom and Dad play billiards. An adult or a child may also wish to steal quietly into the room to use it all by himself—to read, paint, or dream.

Many people use the living room as a common room, and that's fine. For those who wish to set apart a whole room for family where practicality, style, and a homey gemütlich spirit merge, here are some thoughts.

A PLACE FOR YOU, A PLACE FOR ME

It's nice to partition the common room so that varying activities can take place without argument or hassle. Section off areas with portable screens,

This common room is elegant but hardy with durable floors (roll up the Oriental rug for very young children). Fabrics and wall coverings are stain resistant. Many activities can go on at the same time as a family enjoys itself.

Design by Phillip LaBossierre, LaBossierre Associates; photography by Bill Rothschild.

area rugs, and strategically placed furniture. These zones can change according to need. A screen that shields earphone-using music listeners from a teenager doing homework can be taken down when it's time for the disco party.

GOOD LIGHTING

Good lighting alternatives should be available.

- Focused lighting for game tables and hobby areas should provide enough light to cover the widest area.
- Soft, general lighting from indirect sources like wall washers, uplights, portable lamps, or lights behind valances is great for those who wish to watch television or simply relax and talk.
- Reading and other close work requires direct light from lamps or ceiling lights.
- Carefully aimed spotlights to highlight the artwork and other projects that have been created in this very room encourage children and adults to work on *and* display their talents.

A caution: Make sure the cords of table lamps are fastened neatly out of the way, especially if small children will use this room.

A GENTLE-SOUNDING PLACE

An easy, snug ambience really relies on one person's pleasures not encroaching on another's. Here, the trick is to devise reasonable sound-muting measures. You can:

- provide extra sets of earphones for the family stereo or television
- use acoustical tiles on ceilings
- absorb sound with generous carpeting, rugs, and upholstered pieces
- insulate the common room from the rest of the house with a door to keep the noises from one area away from others. If you want to keep your eye on the children, have see-through panes of shatterproof glass installed in the door.

COMMON ROOMS NEED DURABLE FINISHES

Whenever children and adults gather, practicality must reign.

THE FLOOR

Low-pile, easier-to-clean carpeting or roll-up area rugs are one way to go.

Tiled or polyurethaned wood floors are easy to maintain. A decorating tip: Using two solid colors from your favorite sofa or chair fabric, tile a floor or have a wood floor painted checkerboard fashion in those colors. Some pretty combinations, for example: bisque and blue, pale green and soft pink, black and honey.

THE WALLS

Stylish and sophisticated wallpapers that don't resemble the kitschy offerings of years ago are available in washable finishes. If you choose a painted wall, opt for good, high-gloss, washable paint. Wood walls should be spongeable.

THE FABRICS

Choose sturdy materials. Table or furniture covers of stain-resistant cottons, corduroys, and Ultrasuedes, for example, can all be stuffed in the washing machine after the finger-paint spill. Select materials that are formal and pretty enough for adults and versatile enough for the youngest child in the house. Changeable, washable slipcovers and throw pillows with zippered, removable covers are terrific.

Buy extra yardage of the fabric you choose for the adult furniture. Upholster (in zippered slipcovers) large pillows for children's TV lounging or smaller seat pillows for child-sized furniture. Good insurance, too, for emergency recovering of a stained pillow.

COMMON ROOMS NEED VERSATILE FURNITURE

Furniture here should encourage the creative spirit whether that spirit is drawn to finger paints, piano concertos, or high-spirited tangos.

Furniture must be informal and close to indestructible. Glass-topped tables in a common room, for example, should be a definite no. Not only are they dangerous, they are also magnets for fingerprints. Wood, laminates, marble or marble substitutes are more durable. This doesn't mean that the common room must be a bore, or a catchall place for furniture derelicts. It should have a decorating point of view: Design umbrellas *do* come in casual.

Portable furniture makes sense. Nesting tables and pretty foldaway chairs (they're available in marvelous sculptural shapes both in high-tech and traditional materials like bamboo, Lucite, metal, and wood) add form to function. A television and a bar-tea table on wheels, ottomans (with tops that lift for storage), and other upholstered furniture on casters allow people to set up instant corners for themselves.

The common room is a perfect place for a guest sleep sofa, a piano, a Ping-Pong or billiards table, or a beautiful card table that flips open to double its size for easy dining.

Finally, make sure you have enough outlets to plug in the coffeepot and the blender. A plug-in minifridge is also an excellent idea.

COMMON ROOMS NEED WHIMSY AND BEAUTY

Extend your decorating theme in the accessories. Old movie posters or country quilts can be wall art; vintage collections, from miniature chairs to toy locomotives, add personality. The details—the accessories (picture frames, plant containers, table lamps)—of the common room will always enhance charm. Art, including family photographs and children's art, should be well matted, well framed, and well grouped. Wood finishes, color treatments, and rug and walls should relate in pattern and style. Easy-care, worry-free comfort doesn't preclude style.

GOOD STORAGE IS CRUCIAL TO A
WELL-FUNCTIONING COMMON ROOM

Backgammon, chess and checker sets, board games like Scrabble and Monopoly, and pads and pencils all need convenient storage with easy access. Bookcases—built-in or freestanding—cabinets, armoires, and wooden chests are perfect storage. They can house television sets, VCRs, or stereo speakers. *Caution:* Hinged chest lids must be of the type that can't slam down on little fingers.

Attractive wicker baskets to hold bits and pieces of games can be stored in a row on shelves or along a wall. Nests of pretty boxes make attractive storage places. Bicycle baskets on the insides of doors can also hold odds and ends. A small bookcase or storage cabinet near a couch can do double duty as a table surface.

An antique cast-iron stove (they're often found with magnificent hand-painted tiles embedded in the iron) can be transformed into an exquisite bar with room for bottles in the former oven.

A standard clothes closet is inefficient in the common room. Revamp it by first removing the clothes rods, then install shelves for stereo equipment (only the speakers need be in the room proper). Customize your closet with old French baker's racks (originally used to cool breads), which can hold tapes, games, books, and practically everything else. Sturdy, canvas duck tote bags can hang from closet wall hooks. Old camp trunks can live on a closet floor (or anywhere else) to store equipment like racquets or billiard cues.

FINALLY, SPACE

For a cozy ambience, don't fill up every inch. Leave room for caves and dens and dancing.

JUST FOR CHILDREN

While the family room conforms to the needs of children of all ages, a child's room is just his or hers. It is safe harbor. It is cozy incarnate.

All the rules of scale must change. Everything must work from a child's point of view.

All the rules of permanence must change. The room must evolve as the child grows.

Choice Is the First Step

In the room they call "mine," children explore who they are; they create their own real and fantasy worlds—not those of their parents. Giving children choices about the decoration of their own rooms tells them that they have *effect* and they can control their environments. Giving children choice, collaborating with them on room design, gives them a shot of self-esteem and a sense that their input is valued.

Regarding Color

Restrict the choices: Too many options are bewildering. Offer choices within a color spectrum you're comfortable with. Do this by offering color charts with pleasing ranges or by filling a box of crayons with colors that work together. Ask your child to choose a varied selection for his or her room.

Assume nothing: Active, loud, and aggressive children may prefer calming colors like violets, blues, and greens. Shy and quiet children may prefer wake-up colors like yellow, reds, and oranges. The child will know which colors are right for his or her emotional and aesthetic sensibilities—and will tell you, if consulted.

Regarding Size

Crawl around the room on your hands and knees when designing for a small person. See what works for a person who's low to the ground.

- Shelves should be installed so everything is reachable.
- Bookcases should be low easily added to as the child grows.
- Dressers can be enlarged by using modular pieces on top of each other.
- Small tables and chairs for tea parties and finger painting should be Goldilocks-sized.
- Clocks, art, mirrors, and even wall murals should be positioned to be enjoyed by the room's small occupant. Even a wall border should be at the child's head height, not at the wall top. As the child's frame stretches upward, the wall border (called a dado) also should rise. Just this small decorative detail alone keeps the child in proportion to his room.
- Lighting should be at a child's level; retractable suspension cords can hold ceiling fixtures at proper heights, and their levels are adjustable as the child grows.

Room to Grow

Children's rooms should be as expandable as possible. For example, a little girl's trundle bed for sleep-over dates can be converted to deep drawer space when interest in sleep-overs gives way to interest in clothes. A built-in desk surface for a little boy can be first used to display toys. Underneath the wooden desk are wooden toy bins on rollers. In a few years, the toy bins will be gone, leaving the young student with a desk. A bed for a six-year-old may be cozily situated in a corner; underneath the bed, rolling storage carts hold dolls and jump ropes, Crayolas and dinosaurs. As the little girl grows, her teen bed now takes center stage in the room. Gone are the storage bins and added is the organdy princess canopy. Corners that once held dens or caves for quiet playtimes can be converted into dressing rooms or makeup or body-building zones.

STORAGE

Even a closet can be geared for short reaches. The very young can have their clothing hung from rods placed low. As they grow, the rods are raised. Special niches can hold bins for galoshes, shoes, toys, treasures, and other objects the child may need to retrieve.

Cubbies and bins hold the important stuff just within reach of the smaller crowd.
Courtesy of California Closet Co.

Don't equate a tidy room with stowing everything out of view. Children often need their belongings to be seen. Charming hooks can hold pretty hats or party dresses right in view!

As the child grows, rolltop desks can hold school projects safe and intact from day to day. Window seats (with under-the-seat storage), wire baskets, and file cabinets can hold the trappings of youth. And big hooks, screwed into simple strips of wood lining every inch of wall, can hold bicycles, sports equipment, bulletin boards, and even grotesque or unusual collections.

Enormously popular with the young set are old metal school lockers, fitted out with shelves and spray-painted in bright, high-gloss colors. Look for them in junkyards or inquire at schools.

PRIVACY IS VITAL

When siblings share rooms, make sure that attention is paid to the privacy needs of each occupant. Even a small room can be divided by a floor-to-ceiling storage wall, a screen, a two-sided bulletin board, even a colorful cotton spread or a venetian blind hung from a ceiling rod.

DON'T PATRONIZE

The art and other designs you and your children choose should be appropriate to their age but not demeaning. Dumb, kitschy art is not enhancing to anyone's spirit. Wonderful paintings and sculpture can be enjoyed by adults and children alike. Good taste develops from proximity.

COMPACT COZY: FEWER OR SMALLER ROOMS

Cozy seems to be a synonym for compact—but it isn't. Compact rooms can seem tiny and cramped—not comfortably cozy at all—unless you work to make them feel sheltered and snug instead of constricting.

No one ever has enough space and the complaints are legion. The walls are pressing in, if I only had one more room, one more closet, just a drop more breathing space. But you—you who live in that tiny apartment or small house—you *really* have a problem, right?

An astonishingly beautiful, yet ordered and disciplined look can be obtained by making every inch count. Cozy abundance without the downside—the cluttered china-shop effect—is really possible with a little ingenuity and a fresh eye for looking at what already exists.

This is what you want:
- You want your room(s) to stay cozy but *look* bigger.
- You want it all to *feel* cozy and comfortable—not cramped.
- You want storage space.

A *good route to compact cozy is through room zones. A few plush pieces surrounding a dramatic area rug create a sheltering, circular zone.*

Design by Stephen Mallory Associates; photography by Kari Haavisto.

This is how you get it:
- You create double-duty rooms by carving out rooms within rooms. In other words, you harness space within space.
- You rely on visual trickery.
- You buy furniture that does double duty.
- You fall in love with built-ins.

CARVING OUT SPACE

ENLARGE WITH COLOR

Best are monochromatic color schemes (white or off-white) that reflect light and make small spaces seem larger because the eye is allowed to roam uninterrupted around the room. Second best are the cooler colors (green, blue, lavender), which seem to make walls recede, as opposed to the hotter, more intimate colors (reds, oranges, yellows), which, in small quarters, have a limiting effect.

Just as you'd imagine, light colors in fabrics and floors also promote the feeling of space. Window treatments emphasizing sleek rather than fussy—simple floor-length drapes, shoji screens, tailored shades—all in monochromatic shades lend a suggestion of space.

Enlarge with color: Monochromatic white allows the eye to roam, and the space seems stretched.

Design by Bray-Schnaible; photography by François Hollard.

Compact cozy spaces can be created within a larger area. Lightweight, easily installed columns turn a vast space into cozy turfs.

Design by Pasanella & Klein, Stolzman & Berg; photography by Paul Warchol.

ZONE WITH ARCHITECTURE

The natural architecture of a room—floor-to-ceiling beams, alcoves, doors, and windows—can provide easy markers for apportioning areas. If natural dividers don't exist, you can zone by suggestion—you can actually reshape available space with various kinds of imaginative boundary makers. These room dividers not only define and separate living areas, they encourage (or discourage, depending on the need) communication between the areas, allow heat and light to flow through, and anchor activities to given spaces. Sometimes the architecture is permanent (as in a column), sometimes it's movable (as in a long couch), sometimes transparent (as in a glass divider), sometimes opaque (as in a heavy fabric screen). Here are some options:

- screens—fabric screens, screens with clear or etched glass panes to let space-making light shine through; screens with painted or wallpaper scenes to give the illusion of space; shoji screens; mirrored screens; even a "screen" of tall plants all in a row
- columns—either in glass to allow light through or an opaque material to ensure privacy

* half or three-quarter walls, created from a multitude of materials including glass brick and fabric—particularly useful for hiding what you don't want seen, like a washing machine, an old radiator, a pile of dirty laundry, a clothes rack serving as your extra closet.
* wall murals, wallpaper, paint, or varying wall texture to differentiate zones
* furniture placement that sets off and defines one area from another also does the job—a couch placed in the center of a room might create a living zone in front and an office zone in back. Thus, one large room becomes a dining/entertaining/workplace, with the couch acting as a dividing barrier.
* floor-to-ceiling curtains—hung on rods and hooks and made of heavy or gossamer fabric (even beads), make great impromptu "walls."
* area rugs or even an area rug layered on top of wall-to-wall carpeting establish zones within a larger room or try a contrasting border on whatever flooring you have—tile, hardwood, marble, or vinyl—to set one area apart from the other
* low-level lighting in the dining area and a much higher level light in the sitting area automatically separate areas within one room.

Raising the floor with a carpeted wooden platform divides larger space into cozier areas. And, in a small room, raising the floor with another level makes the room seem larger.

Design by Bebe Winkler; photography by Phillip Ennis.

Architecture is a magical presence in space as well as on terra firma. When in doubt about where to go in a small room, raise the floor! Platforms, created of inexpensive wood and covered with the same carpet used throughout the room, give another dimension in space—and the illusion of a separate bedroom, dining or living room. One has to walk up a step to reach the new "room."

Or raise the ceiling! The sky's the limit using self-created architecture. The upper limits of a room don't go to waste when sleep/work balconies or lofts (reachable by an airy ladder) are constructed. These look intricate but are a simple project for a skilled architect or carpenter. By the same token, the lower sections of sleeping platforms can be put to good use with varying levels of built-in storage space.

Finally, use the existing architecture to serve your own purposes. Carve a small dining alcove in an apartment hallway by installing a drop-down, out-of-the-way shelf. Or separate your existing dining room into a three-purpose center where you can eat, hold business meetings, and sleep teenagers. The conference table serves also as dining table; the banquettes used as seating for the dining/conference table can be used as twin beds when needed.

Do It with Mirrors

As any master illusionist knows, mirrors create optical illusions. Trick your guests (and yourself) into seeing *big* where small exists. One way is to find a strategic spot in a room you wish to "widen" and install at least 5 square feet of floor-to-ceiling mirrors on the walls enveloping that spot. This will make the space seem twice as large. Mirrors are indispensable in every room of a very compact home if you want to create visual largesse.

Do It with Multipurpose Furniture (Think About It!)

How many times do you really use a formal dining table? Six, seven times yearly? Do you really need it? Why can't a large desk (which you *do* need) be cleared to serve as an occasional dining table? Add a fabulous cloth, and no one will know the difference. And, if you haven't the room for a formal desk, why not use a narrow table instead, so it also can be pulled into service as a dining table? And why can't your coffee table be adapted to rise in height when guests come over to dine?

Why can't your end tables with the generous shelves under the tops be utilized as extra bookshelves?

Why can't the architectural column you're having built as a room divider be constructed with an "invisible" door that conceals storage shelves in the column's hollow interior?

Why can't a plush, pillow-topped ottoman also serve as a coffee table? And why can't its top open to conceal storage for your tea set—or whatever?

Do it with fakery:
*Trompe l'oeil artistry
gives depth to a flat
wall as beloved objects
are painted onto faux
shelves in a faux niche.*

Design by George Constant,
executed by Creative Art, Inc.

Look what happens when creative planning is applied to a tiny kitchen! Room is found to dine, watch TV, store everything, and even make the table disappear on command. Design by Richard L. Schlesinger, ISID; photography by Bill Rothschild.

Why can't your bed be a Murphy bed, invisibly stored away in the wall until you're ready to dream? And why can't your office or living-room couch be a daybed?

And why can't you use dead space for storage? An old-fashioned sink dressed in an elegant taffeta to-the-floor skirt that conceals everything underneath? A wonderfully decorative chair by the fire serving as an inspired bookshelf (the books are piled up instead of standing side by side)? A dead corner where beautiful nesting tables (available in a variety of styles from American pedigree charm to Italian contemporary chic) can live gracefully and permanently? A rolling work island that stows away under the table in the kitchen with no counter space?

Why not indeed?

DO IT WITH FAKERY

Don't like the brick-wall view from your tiny apartment? How about a mountain in Aspen? Or the Seine? When the walls close in, just pull down a view of wide-open spaces in the form of a trompe l'oeil painting on a wide window shade. Turn a space capsule apartment into a room with a panoramic vista with a choice of oceans, gardens, or whatever makes you feel most cozy-peaceful. And you can keep changing the scenery whenever you like. (See the Resource Guide for artisans.)

DO IT WITH BUILT-INS

When space is limited, built-ins are the answer. Wall-to-wall systems unobtrusively seem to enlarge a room even as they hide entertainment and storage functions. They actually do more than seem to enlarge a room. The walls, which provide the functions of furniture, free up floor space. Custom-designed systems that use every inch by wrapping around windows and corners offer revolving shelves and storage, stereo and television units, roll-top desks and dining surfaces that disappear into the unit when not in use. Anything is possible. If compact cozy is the name of your game, built-ins are your salvation.

AIRY COZY

Picture the scene: Gently, side by side with your friend or lover, you sway on the charming wooden porch swing. Sipping your iced tea on the sunlight-flooded enclosed patio, you've never felt closer to each other. The place is a retreat, both part of and yet removed from the larger world.

Patios, porches, balconies, gazebos, decks—they're all pure gold "rooms" for coziness. But when designed carelessly, they're about as comfortable as miniature public parks. Designed carefully, reaching into the vis-

Airy cozy. A wooden swing can lull anyone into euphoria.

Design by Robert De Carlo Design Associates; photography by Bill Rothschild.

ible or imagined surrounding landscape, they draw upon sky, beach, bay, or even busy city for a sheltered, comfy character.

The trick to airy coziness is *limits*. Outside or see-through enclosed spaces need a definition of boundaries. Consider a beach blanket on the sand. The vast sea and the wide beach surround you, but the blanket defines boundaries, making an intimate and marked-off place for you; it is a snug oasis even on the endless sand.

Although your backyard, deck, or patio is considerably smaller than the beach, it's still out there in the world and thus needs constraints to make it cozy and comfortable. For example, four chairs placed at opposite corners on an open deck don't do it. This placement doesn't suggest a private spot that says "even in the midst of this enormous world, *here* you're safe and comfortable." The chairs must be closer together, turned to one another to define a secluded, even guarded space. This concept is as applicable to a small balcony as it is to the whole backyard.

How else do you create cozy space? You do it with boundary markers like garden statuary, fences, plantings, even night lighting that brings the focus onto people. *Note:* Avoid the "museum effect" in outside lighting—the emphasis of accent spotlights on statuary, plants, or furniture to the exclusion of people. Warm, subtle, sociable lighting humanizes an airy space.

Comfortable outside or enclosed spaces also need easygoing furniture. Ignore stunning but backbreaking styles. Motion furniture is a natural—the nostalgic Adirondack rocker, the womblike rope hammock, swings, and glider lounges that seem to unravel tension with every movement. Stationary chaises, love seats, and wickery club chairs also suggest comfort to many who prefer leaving motion to boats. Pillows should be everywhere, and each seat should have a nearby surface. Side tables are often designed with glass or granite tops because they're airy, durable, and maintenance-easy. If you can't find a table you like, consider placing a glass top on a Corinthian column or even on an old wicker trunk.

Your design umbrella can be extended here, but remember that in airy spaces, casual ought to dominate. Furniture materials are varied. Durable, rust-free aluminum, cast iron, rattan, and wood (teak, redwood, cherry, and mahogany among others) are particularly effective. The fabrics you choose will also reflect your design umbrella: Crisp linens, canvas, and chintzes all come in patterns ranging from cheery florals to more formal and elegant solids and stripes. Throw quilts and pillows can make your furniture chameleonlike, changing with your mood. Check to see that the fabrics are waterproof and mildew resistant if your airy space is open to the elements.

Accessories will bear the stamp of your personal touch. Woven baskets filled with flowering plants or fruits, a stone fountain, an antique birdhouse, an Oriental porcelain garden seat, a sundial, a wheeled cart that serves as a bar/potting shed/dining table—all these extend cozy but airy comfort.

Finally, are you lucky enough to have an overhanging tree to shade your airy spot? Use it as a protective canopy in the sunlight or, studded with tiny lights, to create a twinkling fairyland in the darkness.

TEMPERATURE IN COZY SPOTS

In your niches, nooks, and crannies, your common rooms, your children's rooms, and all your airy places, of course you'll arrange furniture into close, *visually* warm groupings. Still, you must also keep an eye out for physical warmth, a condition that is synonymous with cozy comfort. Family chats and intimate tête-à-têtes go nowhere if even one person feels cold. Apart from turning up the thermostat, here are some tips:

- Take advantage of fireplaces. There's nothing more cozy and conducive to togetherness. If you haven't a built-in fireplace, speak with your contractor about installing a freestanding model.
- Move sheltering love seats and other furniture away from northern or naturally cool walls.
- In the wintertime, move seating groups into the sunlight—nature's own heating system.

In the sultry days of summer, cozy means cool. Lazy overhead fans are a nice alternative to gentle air-conditioning. Outside, leafy bowers and tropical umbrellas provide welcome shelters from the sun.

Feathering a nest: Abundant fabric, fresh flowers, touches of whimsy, and personal mementos feather the comfortable nest.

Design by Teri Seidman Interiors; photography by Bill Rothschild.

VII FEATHERING YOUR NEST

There's more than function and furniture to a wonderfully comfortable home. Watch any bird build her nest. In addition to the bowllike structure usually constructed of mud, the nest would not be complete without the twigs, grasses, and discarded feathers that unify and hold it together. These are the finishing touches, the material that insulates it against the world.

The tiniest sparrow knows how to feather her nest.

And so must we. Indeed, the "feathers" are the fine strokes of decorating and the key to comfort. A place that's too hot, too cold, too dark or light, too garish or dismal, a home that doesn't stick together as a unified whole will not bring that sense of well-being we crave.

MATERIAL COMFORTS

The materials we use to feather the nest—the variously colored and patterned fabrics plus the textures and colors of wall and floor coverings—must balance and complement each other. Whatever your design umbrella—Fine Traditional, Classic Americana, Sleek Contemporary, Regional Flair, or Tranquil Country—you need the "feathers" to pull it all together.

COLOR

Of all the factors that go into making a room feel comfortable, none is so powerful as the use of color. It has affected the level of people's comfort through the ages. The early Native American knew that jarring colors wrecked havoc with tranquillity and so painted his complexion with vivid mineral dyes and clay to frighten off his enemies. Conversely, the ancient Egyptians used light-reflective colored gemstones to evoke healing and mystical comforts in their lives.

It would be a great mistake to ignore color when creating a nurturing, calming home.

It's important to decide on a clear and focused color palette that is appropriate to your design umbrella. Certain colors do seem to characterize specific styles. For example, a French country home reflective of the Empire period traditionally uses particular shades of hyacinth blue with quite wonderful accents of daffodil yellows and creams. Mixing in the barn reds or

A *little paint goes a long way to feather a nest: Sponge-painted walls add intricacy and depth. The rug is a painted illusion.*

Design by Stephanie Stephens Gans Designs Ltd., NYC; photography by Bill Rothschild.

Granny Smith apple greens of a more rustic American country design would not serve the less rugged French country design umbrella.

If your heart sings from the night tones of blues, mauves, and grayed purples with accents of twilight pinks such as might be found in a contemporary city home, reject the sunny yellow accent pillows even though they were an expensive gift. Everytime you look at them, they'll jar your comfort zone.

More thoughts on color:

Warm midtones, ranging from pink tints to creamy peach hues, create a soothing shell for people and environments. These quiet colors flowing across walls and floor (with brighter accents reserved for upholstery) give a *cocoon* effect.

Decide on the emotional effects you wish to achieve. If you want an exercise room to make you feel energized and alive, you may want to fill it with warm reds, yellows, or oranges. On the other hand, if you want to relax in your media room after work, cool colors like blues or green may be more comfortable.

There are many ways to work with color and here are three good options to think about as you begin:

- Choose one hue and use it in various intensities.
- Start by painting everything white or cream and add color and pattern afterward.
- Find a favorite fabric or painting, pull out the colors that make it so comforting to your eye, and use shades of those colors.

Although we all have personal favorites, try to be open-minded: you might just hit on a combination you've never considered before.

How to decide on color?

Some people fall in love with a swatch of material, and the color scheme for a whole room is contained in that tiny suggestion.

Some people choose color schemes from a favorite museum painting or a favorite piece of clothing or even an Oriental rug or Grandmother's old quilt.

Many choose color from nature. Study a honeysuckle flower and see how its yellow merges into a lush cream with blushes of rose or apricot. In a traditional or country home, this combination could inspire pale lemon walls, apricot and rosy peach fabrics, a soft creamy carpet, and accent pillows in shades of the honeysuckle's green leaves. Curtains and blinds might also echo the creamy, peachy flower.

Look at a southwestern desert and see how natural it would be to do a regional living room with sand shades for the dominant floor and wall coverings and splashes of terra-cotta and Indian turquoise in the fabrics and accents.

You may use the colors in the same relative proportion in the room as they appear in the sample you've chosen. For example, the predominant color of the natural object/swatch/rug/dress can be the major color in the room, and a shade of it could be used on the walls, large pieces of upholstery, or the floor. This color can also be echoed in smaller touches throughout the room. Use the brightest, most intense colors as accents on such things as throw pillows, art, and other accessories.

Another way to go is to decorate predominantly within the neutral comfort colors—the beiges, whites, browns, grays and greiges, which are particularly effective under contemporary design umbrellas; or, also quite contemporary, crisp and graphic blacks and whites. Monochromatic color, one color repeated with many gradations of the hue, is especially good for creating a sense of expansiveness in compact rooms.

PATTERNS

A rule of thumb is to choose a pattern that fits the scale of the room. Scale is the size relationship of objects to one another. Furnishings, for example, should relate to the general space as a whole; tiny, delicate chairs seem inappropriate in enormous rooms.

Fabric and wall patterns follow the same rule: Small-scale patterns (there are many exceptions to this rule) generally look better in a smaller room because they make it seem larger. Larger-scale patterns look better in oversized spaces.

Just remember; you can mix and match patterns (plaids with stripes or florals) as long as the mixed patterns relate to each other in color. And varying the size of patterns adds interest; miniprints and maxiflorals are more exciting than miniprints and miniflorals.

TEXTURES

Itchy is never good. Even if it's lovely to look at, it must feel good—or else the whole message of this book is wasted.

In his book *Billy Baldwin Remembers,* the famed designer tells of a client who told him, "I would like to have the sofa covered in a material I've never seen, ideally one that's never been made." When Baldwin asked if she could give him a little hint as to what this texture might be, she replied, "Perhaps one that looks like a lovely little sweater crocheted by old ladies." Maybe, thought Baldwin to himself, he could have the sofa done by the Woman's Exchange. But his client was not dotty—in fact, she was ahead of her time. She wanted to decorate for comfort.

Today, almost anything goes for upholstery texture—anything that feels good to you. Ultrasuede, cashmere, kid, denim, and even kilim rugs are used as often as the more conventional cottons, tapestries or wools and may be treated to resist stains.

Caveat: Durability counts. Fragile, dress-weight fabrics on your couch that look and feel wonderful will not withstand constant use. It's hard to feel comfortable if you're worried about protecting the fabric.

WALLS

Ever since prehistoric man etched charcoal figures on his cave, people have decorated their walls. Nowadays, there are choices other than charcoal.

*Painted faux moldings
provide instant
architecture.*

Design by Teri Seidman Interiors;
photography by Bill Rothschild.

One can paper, cover with fabric, or paint walls, and it isn't even necessary
to do the same thing all over the room. For example:

- Many people zone off an area in a room by papering only one section.
- A smaller surface (like the wall space over the kitchen cabinets) papered or painted in contrast to the rest of the room gives an interesting accent.
- Chair rails or the wall along the rise of the stairwell are places to try decorative edgings.

The wood floor has been painted white. Layered on top is a sisal rug, hand-painted with ribbons and flowers— the ribbons repeated on the floor. A delicate and engaging effect!

Design by Denise Rinfret Interiors, Inc.; photography by Bill Rothschild.

- Painted, stenciled, or wallpaper borders also can provide instant architecture, adding both depth and dimension to boxlike spaces.
- Stenciling, sponged-paint finishes, faux marble or tile, or trompe l'oeil paintings of architectural details (like moldings or dentil trim) give great richness to decor.
- Wood paneling and wainscoting can be especially warm and charming.

A word on ceilings: Ceilings, like walls, can be painted, or covered with fabric or paper, but there's an approach I especially like because it seems to contain and protect a room with great style. I refer to the generous use of fabric on the ceiling in a "tenting" effect. It is just a smashing look!

FLOORS

Hardwood floors are extremely versatile and because they're not machine made, they always project a natural, reassuring warmth. Wood floors also have a resilient surface that's easy on the feet and legs. What's more, wood is a natural insulator, making the floor feel good to the touch. In addition, wood floors can open up a small room or make a large one seem cozy and comfortable. You can choose from a wide variety of woods including oak, cherry, elm, ash, maple, pecan, birch, and beech, each with its own distinctive grain.

Wood floor styles are myriad. Try:
- plank strips for Tranquil Country floors
- pale bleached or painted black-and-white strips for Sleek Contemporary floors
- a parquet for Fine Traditional or Classic Americana floors
- a medley of possibilities for Regional Flair floors.

You can bleach and pickle hardwood flooring for a cheery effect, or create delicate inlays using woods of contrasting colors or grains. Inlays can be used to define the borders of a room or zone it into different areas. Floors can be stenciled with colorful borders or sport eye-catching designs through faux marquetry or other paint effects.

Rugs (or wall-to-wall carpets), tiles, laminates, marble, brick, slate, and terrazzo are other flooring choices, each beautiful in its way. Because individuals differ so much on what feels good underfoot, you must try the floor for comfort before you decide. Some people, for example, find quarry stone or hand-painted ceramic tiles beautiful for kitchen floors but hard on the legs and back. Others love the simple maintenance involved in such flooring so much that they're willing to overlook a small discomfort for the larger comfort of easy care. Many clients opt for resilient vinyl flooring, which is more softly cushioned than ever before.

LAMINATES

They're wonderful for feathering a comfortable nest. Although many designers don't agree, I find them indispensable for solving design problems with built-ins, counter tops, bathroom vanities, and furniture in children's rooms. They're durable, maintenance-magical, and can be very beautiful. New sophisticated colors and finishes make laminates appropriate for the most elegant homes. They include grainy leathers, "antiqued" metallics, and faux marbles and granites. Single patterns create unity and visually expand small spaces, but small and large patterns side by side provide enormous visual interest.

CLIMATE CONTROL

Try feeling comfortable in a freezing cold room or a steamy hot room. Try feeling happy in a room with a perpetual lack of light. Impossible. The light and temperature of our home must be agreeable. While artificial solutions are one possibility, there's a lot to be said for a more natural environment.

WINDOW TREATMENTS

Window treatments play a large part in natural insulation. The lovely news is that today's styles easily serve function. While many still admire heavily draped windows—and indeed these can still be quite magnificent in a Fine Traditional home—the trend is toward a softer, easier window dressing that is more in keeping with American informality.

Windows are quirky, each with its own personality, depending on its shape, size, and who hung it.

A graceful cascade of draperies sets a Grecian tone. A rich, creamy tint is echoed in walls and floor, making an exquisite backdrop for the antique furniture.

Design by Samuel Botero Associates; photography by Dennis Krukowski.

What do you need your window treatments to do?
Keep out drafts?
Keep out heat?
Expose the beautiful view or hide the brick wall?
Temper the glare?
Change the shape of an awkwardly shaped or placed window?
Here are some suggestions you can adapt to your own needs:

BLINDS AND SHUTTERS

Choose from:
- standard roller blinds in a neutral fabric or one complementary to your room decor
- Roman blinds that draw up in broad pleats
- Austrian blinds, scalloped when drawn up
- plastic, metal, or wood venetian blinds
- vertical louver blinds or shutters

CURTAINS

Sheer or opaque, tied back, on window tracks, or poled, the fabric treatment depends on your design umbrella. Just remember, skimpy fabric is never terrific-looking. If you choose to go with curtains, always make them generous, full, and lush, whether they're fragile-sheer or opaque.

Some ways to go:
- Simple curtains can be hung from interesting rods and tied back with beautiful hardware.
- Gathered valances and shirred swags, used alone or topping a gauzy sheer, let in the light as they keep out drafts.
- Double-hung windows look country charming in a plaid or printed gingham gathered as a pull-up balloon or Austrian shade. The shade treatment allows instant access to a view and instant privacy when needed.
- Oddly shaped windows can easily be dealt with both stylistically and functionally. Slanting skylights, round and arched windows, or windows that are too narrow, too diagonal, or too high can be curtained by tacking the hardware right onto the movable window rather than the frame. If you look hard enough, you can usually find hardware designed for pull-down shades on these irregular windows.

INSULATION

Thermal shades are a wonderful invention.

It's easy to seal the edges of windows with duct tape or lengths of foam weather stripping to keep drafts out and heat in. Also consider sealing the draperies to the walls and the outer edge of the windows by sewing Velcro

Oddly shaped windows make architecture and can be covered with originality. These linen shades rise from the bottom, dictating the amount of light: Privacy is ensured while daylight is kept constant.

Design by Bilhuber, Inc.; photography by Oleg March.

or magnetic tape to the drapes and tacking the same material to corresponding places on the wall, then seal fabric to fabric.

THE WINDOW AS ARCHITECTURE

Lately, we've begun to see the window as architecture—to be appreciated and enjoyed instead of being heavily masked. We enjoy the slivers of sunlight dappling our walls, and morning mists add to the general decor of the home. A wonderful approach to such atmospheric climate control combines a delicately light outer fabric over a gossamer window blind. The blind is used only to subdue the brightest morning light. If your windows need heavier insulation to hold the heat in winter and the cool in summer, a heavier treatment is advisable, but translucent blinds that pull up into accordion pleats are a popular choice of the nineties. Used under heavier draperies, these almost invisible blinds translate into a more elegant, formal look while still retaining their versatility.

Bottom line to window treatments: Keep them flexible enough to control glare and heat while making sure you can "lose them" when you want to see the world.

THREE COMFORTING ROUTES TO CLIMATE CONTROL

I know you have air-conditioning and I know you have heat, but consider these old-fashioned approaches to make you feel snug as a bug in a rug:

The cast-iron stove: A potbellied stove, made in new, airtight versions that burn wood with energy-conscious efficiency, brings a fluid, peaceful warmth into almost every room in the house

The fireplace: If your fireplace is boarded up, unboard it. If you have no built-in fireplace, consider installing a freestanding model. A roaring blaze or even glowing embers bring serenity.

The ceiling fan: The fragrances of summer circulate along with the air; gossamer curtains gently ripple; cross breezes are disseminated. Why doesn't everyone have a ceiling fan?

LET THERE BE LIGHT

The key to comfort in lighting is in a balanced system that produces three kinds of illumination:

Ambient lighting—generalized light throughout an area. This is the light you switch on when you enter a room, and it's provided by ceiling or

Let there be light— bold, feathering strokes of light. A variety of light sources—recessed in niches and ceiling and caught in fixtures on the wall and ceiling—give a balanced, glareless level of comfort.

Design by Haverson Rockwell; photography by Paul Warchol.

wall fixtures (including track lights) concealed lights, or floor or table lamps. Floor torchères or wall sconces look marvelous when reflected in a mirror, and lamps can also be a major decorative element. All choices can be found in your favorite material—crystal, bronze, porcelain, ceramic, brass, and a hundred other possibilities.

Task lighting—light directed to a specific surface where a particular task is performed. This is the light aimed at your book. In the living room and bedroom, it's usually provided by table, desk, or floor lamps. In the kitchen, many use fluorescent strips. In the bathroom, a strip of bulbs surrounding the mirror and downlights over baths and basins do the trick.

Accent lighting—directional light used to emphasize a particular object or draw attention to a particular view. This is the light aimed at the portrait over your couch as well as the appealing sculpture on the floor. Various types of spotlights work here, but in particular, uplights and downlights.

If you suffer from frequent eyestrain or fatigue, check to see that you're not subjected to undue glare or too high or too low a level of brightness.

COMFORT CLUES

For two in a bed, make sure each person has an individual task light. Small clip-on lamps that fasten onto night tables or headboards are available in many styles and are as appealing as elegant lamps and the always marvelous wall-mounted Hansen swing-arm lamps.

Pink bulbs warm up and soften any light and make it more flattering. They're particularly effective in white or blue rooms and in table lamps.

Blue and green bulbs have a calming and cooling effect on light; use them in hot weather in rooms you want to make feel shadowy and cool.

Cheer up darker, gloomy rooms during the day with cool, white fluorescent tubes behind window shutters or valances. It looks like natural sunlight filtering through.

Consider filters or gels, which come in varied colors to be fitted over the tops of bulbs. Red makes a room feel cozily comfortable; green makes it cool, dark, and enchanting. The soft surround of colored light encourages loving human contact.

Dimmer switches bring atmosphere, comfort, and accent to any room. Your bedroom needs:
- a soft light to balance the blue haze of the TV screen
- an indirect light to warm intimate moments
- convenient light switches for safe, middle-of-the-night passages
- clear and balanced light for dressing and undressing

Want to make the room seem larger? Try flooding the walls with light from recessed bright bulbs or bulbs on a track about 18 inches to 2 feet out from the wall.

The paisley-quilted table skirt, the delicately fringed lampshade, the charming and carefully arranged art, the button-tabbed draperies, and the cord-embellished chairs are only a few of the elegant details in this Fine Traditional room.

Design by Charlotte Moss; photography by Bill Rothschild.

Want to make the room seem softer? Try uplights in corners. They diffuse the sharp outlines of a room and make the whole space seem gentle.

LET THERE BE DETAILS

The subtle touches, large and small, are what distinguish a room—make it layered, intricate and not merely pretty. It's the details that are intriguing.

LET THERE BE ART

Objects, paintings, collections, or bibelots that define your taste make your home unique. Nothing comforts the mind and heart more than art.

HANG IT

Wall art takes many forms—paintings, photographs, prints, rare objects on pretty shelves, "found" art sculpture (wonderful bleached driftwood, for example), antique-plate collections, tapestries, antique children's furniture, and even a glorious Oriental carpet, too delicate for the floor.

Use your walls with defined and thoughtful creativity. You have a collection of marvelous woven country baskets and you love every one. Piled in the pantry, they're clutter; hung on the wall, they're art. You have a collection of men's headgear—the derby, the panama straw, the hunting cap, the top hat, the ten-gallon cowboy hat. Hung on hooks in a hallway or study, they become a charming, personal statement (and they free up your closet).

Hanging art speaks to strangers but also reminds you who you are. A dress-designer client has watercolor sketches of her favorite designs covering an entire wall. A writer has framed the jackets of the foreign language editions of her books dominating her office wall.

TIP: Rotate the wall hangings from time to time. It keeps your home an ever-changing delight.

DISPLAY IT ON A SURFACE

Collections: Groups of objects make an attractive art display. Eight antique porcelain frogs deftly placed together on a green damask-skirted table are infinitely more wonderful than eight porcelain frogs scattered throughout the room. Groups of silver-framed portraits of early ancestors, a pipe collection, or a gathering of inlaid boxes lend cachet when displayed together, and are lost when distributed singly throughout the room.

Single Objects on a Flat Surface: Make sure each is perfectly beautiful or perfectly interesting.

Let there be art:
One enormous
contemporary canvas
sets the stage for a sleek
design umbrella. Art is
the most beautiful nest
feather.

Design by Carl D'Aquino;
photography by Guy Lindsay.

HAVE A UNIFYING LINK

A collection of early French ironstone holds together because it's connected by color, size, and material. Artistic objects on the wall should also bear a relationship to one another. A wall filled with several botanical prints, several turn-of-the-century samplers, or several ancestor portraits is more interesting than a wall dotted with one botanical print, one sampler, and one lonely ancestor.

USE YOUR USABLE ART

An antique nineteenth-century Russian silver samovar can stand stupidly taking up space, expecting to be admired or it can function as a flower container or part of a tea service. A valuable majolica bowl can stand uselessly on a surface or it can hold dried flower petals or candy. Objets d'art somehow seem far more exquisite when they are pressed into service.

DEFINE YOUR DESIGN UMBRELLA

Art doesn't have to be "all of a style," naturally, but it certainly can refine and define a look. Beribboned, gilt-framed botanical prints add immeasurably to a Tranquil Country room. Formal portraits of dogs or ancestors lend authenticity to a Fine Traditional decor. Dramatic abstracts complement a Sleek Contemporary design umbrella.

SCALE AND RELATION

Keep scale in mind: A huge piece of art must be balanced by furnishings that are large enough to carry it. A sculpture should command attention—no matter how small or large.

Different pictures can relate to one another if they are framed the same way, perhaps all in brass, wood, or chrome or all matted in the same color.

LOVE IT

You must be in love with your art—or don't hang or display it. Nothing comforts the mind and heart more than cherished art.

LET THERE BE CHOICE

Every bird chooses the feathers she admires to fluff up her nest. Some like it full, some like it spare. Be open to the influences of the wide world and take your comfort where you find it. If the idea of a pillowed, ebullient, Russian-red, furniture-rich room brings you harmony—take it home. If the idea of a simple, mystical serenity brings you peace, take it home.

LET THERE BE PILLOWS

Nothing feathers the nest more lushly than pillows; use them lavishly.

LET THERE BE PETS

Living with small furry or feathered creatures shouldn't produce angst and aggravation. Here are some suggestions for comfortable coexistence.

THE FLOOR

Carpeting is not the best choice for obvious reasons, but if you go that route, ask the carpet company how to remove stains. A patterned carpet will show fewer stains than a solid color.

Area rugs that can be rolled up and cleaned are a better bet. They can look beautiful on wood, tile, or marble floors.

Or paint the floor to fit under your design umbrella.

FABRIC

Nubby upholstery fabric on furniture catches dog and cat claws. A better choice is smooth weaves.

Pet hairs don't cling to smooth fabrics as readily as they do to deeper piles.

If your pet insists on using your best chair as his snooze spot, protect it with an extra piece of the same fabric, which can be removed for company.

It's not insane to think about matching furniture fabrics to your pet's color: Hairs show far less. Light colors (certainly white) should be eschewed for dirty-paw reasons.

OTHER TIPS

Ask the pet store about nontoxic, odor-free sprays to discourage your pet from using or chewing the furniture.

Litter boxes are unsightly, even if one owns a fastidious cat. If you have a pedestal sink, a pretty skirt creates a privacy haven for the cat and hides the box from you. You can also convert an under-the-sink vanity into a niche for a litter box by installing a small door the cat can open at will.

If you have a bird, make sure there's a large tray somewhere under the cage to catch birdseed and feathers that come through the bars of the cage.

That bird should be in a gilded cage—or at least, the most beautiful cage you can find. Marvelously ornate antiques and reproductions abound. Dog and cat beds can be upholstered in the same fabric you use on couches or for bedspreads. It makes for a nice touch!

RETURN TO NATURAL

soothing
environment-friendly
natural

These are the code words of the generation that is making a mass retreat home again. The urge to feather one's nest with things that are real, unprocessed, pure, nontoxic, and energy-conserving is a lovely outgrowth of our raised consciousness about a safer planet.

Furniture in unfinished pine or maple, wicker, rattan, bamboo, twig, or log; sisal rugs, rush matting, wood, stone, and slate floors; handwoven all-wool or cotton throws and blankets; natural potpourri, pungent cedar blocks, fresh and dried flowers; unbleached fabrics; energy-efficient light bulbs; nontoxic paints—all these signal a return to our roots, an indoor extension of all that is natural and good outdoors.

Let us feather our nests naturally when we can.

Epilogue: The Onion Theory

It is a complicated thing, comfort.

Describing it is like trying to describe an onion, says the brilliant philosopher Witold Rybczynski. An onion appears simple on the outside but how deceptive that is! With its many translucent layers, an onion is profoundly complex.

Comfort is also an intricate concept with many layers of meaning—privacy, ease, convenience—some of which are obvious and some of which are buried deep. Further, when we try to describe individual layers of either an onion or comfort, it's easy to lose sight of the whole.

What are some of the layers? Decorating for comfort must include convenience (a handy table), efficiency (a great light), domesticity (a cozy common room), physical ease (a cushioned chaise), and privacy (a niche, a nook, or a cranny for a talk or a great read).

It can also mean rethinking the structure of familiar rooms. Who says a bathroom can't be a haven of relaxation, as it is in Japan, a room filled with charm and privacy that's ensured by creative placement of fixtures? Who says a kitchen must have work surfaces of standardized height and width, all uniformly finished in the same material? Who says a living room is just for company?

Pure comfort should mean chairs that are less an artistic statement and more a pleasure to sit in, a new emphasis on intimacy, room layouts that make more sense than they do now, and above all, devotion to function. Things must *work* for your ease.

Comfort, like an onion, defies an easy analysis.

But think of it: Once we get the hang of the onion theory, once we begin to pay attention to the many nuances of comfort—anything is possible! And then, as Sir Walter Scott said, "Let it freeze without: we are comfortable within."

There's no place like home,
If . . . it feels good.

RESOURCE GUIDE

ADDRESSES AND
INFORMATION BEGIN
ON PAGE **186.**

CHAPTER III: VOLUPTUOUS COMFORT

BEDS
Alice's Antiques (antique iron)
American Roots (twig)
Avery Boardman (sleep sofas)
Benicia Foundry & Iron Works (metal beds)
Bramson House (upholstered headboards)
Charles Beckley & Sons (upholstered headboards)
Councill Craftsmen (Fine Traditional)
Daniel Mack (tree branches)
Gary Buxbaum Co., Ltd. (custom upholstery)
Ligne Roset (wildly contemporary)
Lorraine Furniture Co. (quick-change fabric)
Newel Art Galleries, Inc. (fine antiques)
Shannon & Jeal (iron beds)
Williamsburg Reproductions (Classic Americana)

LINENS
Bramson House (bedspreads)
Chambers (catalog)
D. Porthault, Inc. (premier)
E. Braun & Co., Inc. (luxury)
Faribo Co. (blankets)
Françoise Nunnalé (antique)
Gazebo of New York (country quilts)
Hand Made Quilts (Amish quilts)
Lerón (lavish)
Martex (bed and bath)
Polo Ralph Lauren (coordinates)
Pratesi (upscale)
Scandia Down (catalog)

Thief River Linens (custom)
Upstairs Down Shop (comforters)
Utica (bed and bath)

HIDDEN COMFORTS
California Closets (organizers)
E. R. Carpenter Co., Inc. (convoluted mattress pads)
Flex-A-Bed (motorized mattresses)
Pure Podunk, Inc. (organic bedding)
Roloke Co. (therapeutic neck pillows)
Sealy, Inc. (water beds)
Select Comfort Sleep Systems (air mattresses)
White Home Products, Inc. (closet carousel)

EXERCISE/SPA
Life Fitness, Inc. (stationary bicycles)
NordicTrack (home gym)
Sharper Image (catalog)
Stairmaster (stair climbers)
Studio East Exercise Center (consultant)
Trotter (treadmills)

CHAPTER IV: SOCIAL COMFORT

CLASSIC AMERICANA
E. J. Audi (Mission reproductions)
Ethan Allen
Frederick Duckloe & Bros., Inc. (Windsor chairs)
L. & J. G. Stickley, Inc. (Mission reproductions)
Williamsburg Reproductions
Winterthur Museum & Gardens

FINE TRADITIONAL
Bombay Company (reproductions)
Brunschwig & Fils (upholstered French)
Councill Craftsmen (mahogany)
Decorator's Walk (eclectic)
Girard-Emilia (fine reproductions)
Harden Furniture Company
Ian Harrington (Anglo Raj)
John Rosselli (antiques)
John Widdicomb (Mario Buatta collection)
La Barge (mirrors and brass)
Niermann Weeks Company (iron)
Old Town Crossing (English antiques)
Ritter Antik (Biedermeier)
Sentimento (antique accessories)

SLEEK CONTEMPORARY
Anchor Concepts
Atelier International
Bernhardt Furniture Co.
Chromcraft Furniture Corp.
Dakota Jackson
Deco Deluxe (antiques)
Herman Miller, Inc. (Eames chair)
IPF International (Barcelona chair)
Ligne Roset
Museum of Modern Art Design Store
Norsk, Inc. (Stressless chair)
Pace Collection
Palazzetti

REGIONAL FLAIR
ABC Carpet & Home (southwestern plus)
Arte de Mexico
Cedar Hill (Adirondack chair)
Lane Furniture Company (southwestern plus)
Orchid Island Trading Co. (southeastern)
Quogue Emporium (seaside)
S. T. Preston & Son, Inc. (nautical)
Southwest Gallery
Zona (southwestern plus)

TRANQUIL COUNTRY
American Roots (twig)
Antiques Center at the Mill
Bielecky Bros., Inc. (fine wicker)
Daniel Mack (rustic)
Gazebo of New York (patchwork quilts)

Lane Furniture Co.
Masterworks (accessory catalog)
Palacek (wicker)
Pea Ridge Purities (country crafts)
Shannon & Jeal (iron)
Thonet Industries (bentwood rocker)

CHAPTER V: HIGH-FUNCTION COMFORT

BATHS
American Standard Co. (fixtures)
David Jae & Co. (heat mat)
Davis & Warshow, Inc. (fixtures)
Epánel, Inc. (heated towel bars)
Hastings Tile & Il Bagno (fixtures)
Home Depot (remodeling products)
Jacuzzi Whirlpool Bath (showers, too)
Kohler Co. (fixtures)
Kraft Hardware
Mr. Steam (steam showers)
Paul Associates (fine faucets)
Soft Bathtub Co.

KITCHENS
Delta Faucet Co.
Emerson Electric Co. (Insta-Hot)
Formica Corporation
Grohe America, Inc. (faucets)
Jenn-Air Company (cooktops)
KWC/WSWC (faucets)
Magic Chef (ranges)
Speakman (automatic faucets)
Williams-Sonoma (accessories)

HOME OFFICE
Back Care Corporation (computer helpers)
Backsaver Products Co. (kneeling chair)
Bevan Funnell Ltd. (computer desk)
Duane Moerke (slide-out keyboard drawer)
Fairington Company (leather furniture)
47 St. Photo (machines)
La-Z-Boy Chair Co. (executive recliner)
PML Furniture Group (ergonomic chairs)
Reliable Home Office (catalog)
Sauder Woodworking (office furniture)
Staples (office supplies)
Vecta (chairs)

MEDIA
A.D.S. Multi-Room Systems (remote-control sound)
Audio Video Craft (installers)
Auton Company (automatic lifts)
Bang & Olufsen of America (components)
Faroudja System (video amplifier)
Nouvel Space (installers)
Phoenix Systems (installers)
Revox America, Inc. (speakers)
Sharp Electronics Corporation
Siedle (intercoms)
Sound Advance Systems (speakers)

CHAPTER VI: COZY COMFORT

COMMON ROOM COZY
Blatt Bowling & Billiard Co.
Play Master-Renaissance (billiard tables)
Yamaha Corporation of America (player piano)

CHILDREN COZY
Child Craft Industries, Inc. (Crib 'n Bed)
Children's Furniture Company (educational furniture)
Children's Room, Inc. (Scandinavian)
Country Folk (quilts)
Gil Associates (contemporary)
Hold Everything (storage accessories)
Juvenile Lifestyles, Inc. (castle bunk bed)
Thank Heaven for Little Ones (whimsical)

COMPACT COZY
Avery Boardman (sleep sofas)
Interform (contemporary furniture)
Ligne Roset (contemporary furniture)
Murphy Door Bed Co.
Museum of Modern Art Design Store (folding cart)

AIRY COZY
Barlow Tyrie, Inc. (garden furniture)
Brown Jordan (outdoor furniture)
Gardener's Eden (accessories)
Smith & Hawken (hammocks)
Triconfort (outdoor wicker)
Tropitone Furniture Co. (patio furniture)

CHAPTER VII: FEATHERING YOUR NEST

FABRICS
Brunschwig & Fils (French)
Clarence House (English)
Custom Laminations, Inc. (quilting and plasticizing)
F. Schumacher & Co. (wide variety)
Laura Ashley (English country)
Scalamandré (Fine Traditional)
Ultrasuede (man-made suede)
Waverly, Inc. (popular priced)

WALLS
Benjamin Moore & Co. (paint)
Chevalier (fine tapestries)
Christopher Hyland (wallpaper borders)
Pir Imports (reproduction tapestries)
Pittsburgh Corning Corp. (glass block)
Quik-Trak, Inc. (fabric mountings)

FLOORS
American Olean (tiles)
Porcelanosa (tiles; walls, too)
Shyam Ahuja (area rugs)
Stark Carpets (custom)
Yankee Pride (rag rugs)

CLIMATE CONTROL
Emerson Electric Co. (thermostats)
Glass Tech Services, Inc. (Scotchtint installers)
Heat-N-Glo (gas fireplaces)
Honeywell, Inc. (home control systems)
Hunter Fan Co. (ceiling fans)
Marvin Windows (remote-control windows)
Phifer Wire Products (awning fabrics)
Solar Screen (translucent shades)
Somfy Systems, Inc. (awning controls)
3M Energy Control Products (sun-control film)
Vermont Castings (woodstoves)
Woodstock Soapstone Co., Inc. (woodstoves)

Window Treatments

Appropriate Technology Co. (window quilts)
G & G Concepts, Ltd. (custom draperies)
Hunter-Douglas (Duette shades)
Joanna Western Mills Co. (shutters)
Joseph Biunno (drapery hardware)
Lun On Company (matchstick shades)
Medina Decorators, Inc. (custom draperies)
Nanik (wooden blinds)
Rue de France (lace panels)
Vesta Inc. (drapery hardware)
Window Modes (custom treatments)

Lighting

American Glass Light Co.
Frederick Cooper (lamps)
Hinson Co, (Hanson swing-arm lamp)
Thomas P. Richmond, Inc. (lighting design)

Artisans, Craftspeople, and Contractors

Building Block (custom cabinetry)
Creative Art, Inc. (faux finishes)
Dan Boster (house painting)
David Mims (house painting)
Design & Renovation Consortium
JoAnne Amos (faux finishes)
John P. Meyer & Sons (contractor)
Morton Books (interior design bookstore)
Patrick Clark (etched glass)
Period Details, Inc. (decorative painting)
Sears & Sears (architects)
Seatuck Electric (electrical contractor)
Tromploy, Inc. (trompe l'oeil)

Pillows

Cachet (vintage pillows)
Pillow Finery (custom pillows)
Terry L. Morton (fine antique)
Thimbelina (needlepoint)

More Creature Comforts

American Massage (vibrating chairs)
Armstrong World Industries, Inc. (acoustical ceilings)
Aromatique (home fragrances)
BarcaLounger Reclining Chair
Eli Wilner (period frames)
Faces of Time (antique accessories)
Fiber-Seal International (fabric protector)

Hammacher Schlemmer (accessories)
Jeffrey Aronoff, Inc. (throws)
Kraft Hardware
La-Z-Boy Chair Co.
North Shore Weavers (throws)
Seventh Generation (ecological products)
Stark Lobster & Marine Systems (fish tanks)
Treadles, N.Y. (throws)
Vermont Teddy Bear Co.

Consumer Information Councils

American Lighting Association
435 North Michigan Avenue, Suite 1717
Chicago, IL 60611
800-BRIGHT IDEAS

American Society of Interior Designers (ASID)
National Headquarters
608 Massachusetts Avenue, NE
Washington, DC 20002
212-546-3480

Architectural Woodwork Institute (AWI)
2310 S. Walter Reed Drive
Arlington, VA 22206

Custom Electronic Design and Installation Association (CEDIA)
10400 Roberts Road
Palos Hills, IL 60465
708-598-7070

Hardwood Manufacturers Association
400 Penn Center Blvd.
Pittsburgh, PA 15235
800-373-WOOD

International Furnishings & Design Association (IFDA)
New York Chapter
200 Lexington Avenue, #222
New York, NY 10021
212-686-6020

ISABEL O'NEIL SCHOOL FOR THE
ART OF THE PAINTED FINISH ,
177 East 87 Street
New York, NY 10128
212-348-2120

JUVENILE PRODUCT
MANUFACTURERS ASSOCIATION
2 Greentree Center
Marlton, NJ 08053
609-985-2878

NATIONAL ASSOCIATION OF THE
REMODELING INDUSTRY (NARI)
1901 North Moore St., Suite 808
Arlington, VA 22209
703-276-7600

NATIONAL DECORATING PRODUCTS
ASSOCIATION (NDPA)
1050 North Lindbergh Blvd.
St. Louis, MO 63132-2994
314-991-3470

NATIONAL HOME FURNISHINGS
ASSOCIATION (NHFA)
305 West High Street
High Point, NC 27261
800-888-9590

NATIONAL KITCHEN & BATH
ASSOCIATION (NKBA)
687 Willow Grove Street
Hackettstown, NJ 07840
908-852-0033

Resources: Code and Pertinent Information

ABC Carpet & Home
888 Broadway
New York, NY 10003
212-473-3000
   Furnishings include handwoven Navajo wool rugs and primitive-looking southwestern furniture. (R)

ADS Multi-Room Systems
One Progress Way
Wilmington, MA 01887
800-522-4434
   Highest-quality sound-control system that allows access from all rooms. (M)

Alice's Antiques
505 Columbus Avenue
New York, NY 10024
212-874-3400
   Large selection of authentic antique iron beds. (R)

American Glass Light Co.
9 West 27 Street
New York, NY 10001
212-213-1200
   Stunning collection of coordinated lighting fixtures, including hanging lights and sconces. (M)

American Massage
341 Central Avenue
Silver Creek, NY 14136
716-934-2648
   Reclining chair with heat and massage units. (M)

American Olean
1000 Cannon Avenue
Lansdale, PA 19446
215-855-1111
   Popular-priced domestic tiles in a wide variety of colors, shapes, and sizes for mixing and matching. (M)

American Roots
PO Box 2462, Route 47
New Preston, CT 06777
   Handcrafted willow twig beds, chairs and tables. (C)

American Standard Co.
40 West 40 Street
New York, NY 10016
800-821-7700, Ext. 4023
   Comfortably proportioned bath and kitchen fixtures and hardware. (M)

Anchor Concepts
500 Nepperhan Avenue
Yonkers, NY 10701
914-965-5020
   Custom cabinetry for media and storage. (D)

Antiques Center at the Mill
164 Montauk Highway
Westhampton, NY 11977
516-288-0206
   Huge landmark building chock-full of imported country French armoires, bedroom sets, dining tables, and servers. (R)

APPROPRIATE TECHNOLOGY CO.
Old Ferry Road
Brattleboro, VT 05301
802-257-4501
Cozy window quilts that insulate better than three layers of glass, drastically lowering heat loss. (M)

ARMSTRONG WORLD INDUSTRIES, INC.
PO Box 3001
Lancaster, PA 17604
800-233-3823
Acoustical control ceiling panel and grid system. Vinyl tile and sheet resilient flooring. (M)

AROMATIQUE
PO Box 309, Highway 25 N
Heber Springs, AR 72543
800-262-7511
Fragrances for the home, potpourri, and a charming scented Mario Buatta bear. (M)

ARTE DE MEXICO
5356 Riverton Avenue
North Hollywood, CA 91601
878-769-5090
Array of southwestern handmade furniture, light fixtures, and accessories. (C)

ATELIER INTERNATIONAL
235 Express Street
Plainview, NY 11803
516-935-6700
Noted architect-designed contemporary classic furniture, including that of Frank Lloyd Wright. (D, M)

AUDIO VIDEO CRAFT
37-22 30th Street
Long Island City, NY 11101
718-706-8300
Designs, supplies and installs state-of-the-art home entertainment systems, including home theaters and multiroom remote-control audio systems. (I)

AUTON COMPANY
Box 1129
Sun Valley, CA 91353-1129
818-367-4340
Electronic pop-up lifts for TVs, computers, bars, and stereos; motorized TV swivel units. (M)

AVERY BOARDMAN
979 Third Avenue
New York, NY 10022
212-688-6611
Custom sleep sofas and upholstered headboards. (D, M)

BACK CARE CORPORATION
200 S. Desplaines Avenue
Chicago, IL 60661
312-258-0888
Distributor of computer products for greater comfort, including Swivel Wrist/Arm Supports, the UnMouse, a touch tablet to avoid wrist movements, and the E-Z View computer monitor hood for bifocal wearers. (C)

BACKSAVER PRODUCTS CO.
53 Jeffrey Avenue
Holliston, MA 01746
800-251-2225
MA: 508-429-5940
Orthopedically designed seating for the home and office, including swivel kneeling chairs. (C, M)

BANG & OLUFSEN OF AMERICA
1150 Feehanville Drive
Mount Prospect, IL 60056
312-299-9380
Elegantly designed state-of-the-art television and stereo equipment. (M)

BARCALOUNGER RECLINING CHAIR
1450 Atlantic Avenue
Rocky Mount, NC 27802
919-977-6395
Popular-priced recliner and modular reclining units. (M)

BARLOW TYRIE, INC.
65 Great Valley Parkway
Malvern, PA 19355
800-451-7467
English teak garden furniture, specializing in tree seats and benches. (M)

BENICIA FOUNDRY & IRON WORKS
720 East H Street
Benicia, CA 94510
707-745-4645
Brass, painted, and iron beds, including trundles. (M)

BENJAMIN MOORE & CO.
Chestnut Ridge Road
Montvale, NJ 07645
201-573-9600
Paints and stains for interior and exterior use. (M)

BERNHARDT FURNITURE CO.
PO Box 740
Lenoir, NC 28645
704-758-9811
Chic upholstered modular seating with tilting backs and hidden footrests for "easy chair" reclining. (M)

BEVAN FUNNELL LTD.
200 Lexington Avenue
New York, NY 10016
212-683-0380
Mahogany high/low remote-control desk to conceal computer. (M, D)

BIELECKY BROS., INC.
306 East 61 Street
New York, NY 10021
212-753-2355
Top-of-the-line rattan, cane, and wicker furniture, including beds and headboards. (M)

BLATT BOWLING & BILLIARD CO.
809 Broadway
New York, NY 10003
212-674-8855
Antique and handcrafted reproduction billiard tables. (R)

BOMBAY COMPANY
550 Bailey, Suite 400
Fort Worth, TX 76107-2110
800-535-6876
Affordable eighteenth- and nineteenth-century English reproductions, including tea tables, lingerie chests, desks, and versatile banquet table that folds to game size and then console. Chain. (C, R)

BRAMSON HOUSE
5 Nassau Street
Rockville Centre, NY 11570
516-764-5006
Custom outline quilted bedspreads, draperies, headboards. Popular priced. (C)

BROWN JORDAN
9860 Gidley Street
El Monte, CA 91734
213-686-0951
Fine outdoor furniture, including comfort chaises and dining sets. (M)

BRUNSCHWIG & FILS
979 Third Avenue
New York, NY 10022
212-838-7878
Distinctive French fabrics and lovely custom upholstered furniture. (D)

BUILDING BLOCK
314 Eleventh Avenue
New York, NY 10001
212-714-9333
Quality traditional and contemporary architectural woodworking, cabinetry, and furniture, custom-designed and engineered to specific requirements. (A)

CACHET
Box 1035
Manchester Center, VT 05255
802-362-0058
Limited-edition decorative pillows from vintage fabrics, ribbons, and braids. (M, R)

CALIFORNIA CLOSETS
17 Montgomery Street, #249
San Francisco, CA 94111
415-433-9999
Custom closet organizers. National chain. (I)

CEDAR HILL
210 Northwestern Avenue
West Bend, WI 53095
800-841-5581
Classic American Adirondack chair and footrest crafted from red cedar. (M, C)

CHAMBERS
PO Box 7841
San Francisco, CA 94120-7841
800-334-9790
Lavish linens and accessories for bed and bath. (C)

CHARLES BECKLEY & SONS
306 East 61 Street
New York, NY 10021
212-759-8450
Custom upholstered headboards, daybeds, and trundles. (D)

CHEVALIER
11 East 57 Street
New York, NY 10022
212-750-5505
Exquisite centuries-old tapestries for feathering your nest in true castle style. (R, D)

CHILD CRAFT INDUSTRIES, INC.
501 E. Market Street
Salem, IN 47167
812-883-3111
Originator of convertible Crib 'n Bed with built-in storage. Attractive tot-to-teen furniture. (M)

CHILDREN'S FURNITURE COMPANY
1234 Leadenhall Street
Baltimore, MD 21230
410-625-7908
Tables and chairs as learning devices: Carved and painted botanically correct leaves serve as chair backs. (M, D)

CHILDREN'S ROOM, INC.
318 East 45 Street
New York, NY 10017
212-687-3868
Scandinavian furniture for young people: bunk beds, wall units, desks. (R)

CHRISTOPHER HYLAND
979 Third Avenue
New York, NY 10022
212-688-6121
Oustanding wallpaper borders and coordinates. Splendid fabrics. (D)

CHROMCRAFT FURNITURE CORP.
1 Quality Lane
Senatobia, MS 38668
601-562-8203
Casual dining and game furniture with chairs that tilt, swivel, and roll. (M)

CLARENCE HOUSE
211 East 58 Street
New York, NY 10022
212-752-2890
Richly designed English fabrics. (D)

COUNCILL CRAFTSMEN
Box 398
Denton, NC 27239
704-869-2155
Beautifully carved eighteenth-century English and American furniture reproductions. (M)

COUNTRY FOLK
Rocky Point Road
Rowayton, CT 06853
203-655-6887
Crib quilts in classic patchwork designs. (C)

CREATIVE ART, INC.
333 East 69 Street
New York NY 10021
212-517-7658
Decorative artist for murals and faux finishes on walls and furniture. (A)

CUSTOM LAMINATIONS, INC.
932 Market St., PO Box 2066
Paterson, NJ 07509
201-279-9174
   Send fabrics for: vinylizing, flame retardancy, Tyvek backing, paperbacking, and quilting by the yard. (C)

D. PORTHAULT, INC.
18 East 69 Street
New York, NY 10021
212-688-1660
   Premier linens with Continental styling. (R)

DAKOTA JACKSON
306 East 61 Street
New York, NY 10021
212-838-9444
   Museum-recognized stylish contemporary furniture, including compact bar. (M, D)

DAN BOSTER
145 East 17 Street, #A-5
New York, NY 10003
212-673-3002
   Quality painting and wallpapering. (A)

DANIEL MACK
225 West 106 Street
New York, NY 10025
212-866-5746
   Designer twig, branch, and root furniture, which includes daybeds, headboards, tables, and chairs. (A, C)

DAVID JAE & CO.
519 South Fifth Avenue
Mount Vernon, NY 10550
914-664-8282
   Heat mats for installation under tile floors. (M)

DAVID MIMS
725 Taylor Street
East Patchogue, NY 11772
516-281-5815
   Interior and exterior custom painting company. (A)

DAVIS & WARSHOW, INC.
150 East 58 Street
New York, NY 10022
212-593-0435
   Bath fixtures by Kohler, American Standard, and Kallista. (D)

DECO DELUXE
1050 Second Avenue
New York, NY 10022
212-751-3326
   Upscale, one-of-a-kind Art Deco furnishings. Antiques, no catalog. (D, R)

DECORATOR'S WALK
979 Third Avenue
New York, NY 10022
212-319-7100
   Showroom featuring an exceptional array of custom furniture. (D)

DELTA FAUCET CO.
55 East 111 Street
Indianapolis, IN 46280
317-848-1812
   Kitchen and bath antiscald faucets and showers, gourmet spray faucets. (M)

DESIGN & RENOVATION CONSORTIUM
136 East 56 Street
New York, NY 10022
212-673-2100
   Cooperative of independent designers and contractors for expert execution of projects. (A)

DUANE MOERKE
Phone orders only
612-881-4404
   Slide-out keyboard drawer that goes under the desk and drops the typing height by 3 inches. (M, R)

E. BRAUN & CO., INC.
717 Madison Avenue
New York, NY 10021
212-838-0650
   Heirloom-quality bed and bath linens. (R)

E. J. AUDI
160 Fifth Avenue
New York, NY 10010
212-679-7580
Authentic reproductions of Stickley Mission Oak furniture. (R)

ELI WILNER
1525 York Avenue
New York, NY 10028
212-744-6521
Period frames for fine art and mirrors. (D, R)

EMERSON ELECTRIC CO.
9797 Reavis Road
St. Louis, MO 63123
314-577-1412
Residential thermostats, programmable for heat/cooling, whole-house electronic air cleaners. In-Sink-erator garbage disposals and Insta-Hot hot water dispenser. (M)

EPÁNEL
PO Box 115
145 Route 31
Pennington, NJ 08534
609-466-1172
Heated towel bars. (R)

E. R. CARPENTER CO., INC.
5016 Monument Avenue
Richmond, VA 23230
800-225-4942
Support pillows, neck pillows, convoluted mattress pads, chiropractic pillows. (M)

ETHAN ALLEN
Ethan Allen Drive
Danbury, CT 06811
203-743-8000
Nicely styled traditional furniture sold nationwide. Chain. (R)

F. SHUMACHER & CO.
979 Third Avenue
New York, NY 10022
212-415-8800
Excellent fabrics, ranging from documentary prints to contemporary wovens. (D, M)

FACES OF TIME
32 West 40 Street
New York, NY 10018
212-921-0822
Delightful antique accessories for old-fashioned comfort and style. By appointment. (D)

FAIRINGTON COMPANY
PO Box 3827
Hickory, NC 28603
800-345-1777
Reasonably priced fine-quality upholstered leather sleepers, lounge chairs, ottomans, and swivel executive desk chairs. (M)

FARIBO CO.
1500 NW Second Avenue
Faribault, MN 55021
507-334-6444
Blankets and throws in the finest wools, mohair, merino, blends, and cottons, including Supima, combed, and Upland, as well as acrylics and blends. (M)

FAROUDJA SYSTEM
675 Palomar Avenue
Sunnyvale, CA 94086
408-735-1492
Enhances video signals—creates an image whose appearance is closer to film and HDTV. (M)

FIBER-SEAL INTERNATIONAL
10755 Sanden Avenue
Dallas, TX 75238
214-349-8374
Seals and protects fabric and rug fibers in the home for easy removal of stains. (I)

FLEX-A-BED
PO Box 7500
Long Beach, CA 90807
800-421-2277
Motorized mattresses, which can include vibration massage features, individual adjustment in king/queen. (M)

FORMICA CORPORATION
10155 Reading Road
Cincinnati, OH 45241
800-SAMPLES
Developer of hard-surface material used for countertops and furniture. Call for brochures and recommendations for applications. (M)

47 ST. PHOTO
67 West 47 Street
New York, NY 10036
212-398-1410
Well-stocked discount electronics store. (R)

FRANÇOISE NUNNALLÉ
105 West 55 Street
New York, NY 10019
212-246-4281
Exquisite antique one-of-a-kind bed linens and toss pillows. By appointment. (D, R)

FREDERICK COOPER
2545 West Diversey
Chicago, IL 60647
312-384-0800
Wide variety of lamps, including the Mario Buatta English country collection. (M)

FREDERICK DUCKLOE & BROS., INC.
PO Box 427
Portland, PA 18351
717-897-6172
Fine crafted Windsor chairs, including Executive Tilt swivels, First Boston rockers, and Gentlemen's Windsor Rockers. (M, C)

G & G CONCEPTS, LTD.
315 Hudson Street
New York, NY 10013
212-741-3899
Fine custom draperies to the trade. (D)

GARDENER'S EDEN
PO Box 7307
San Fancisco, CA 94120-7307
800-822-9600
The sturdy Falcetti umbrella, umbrella lights, snack caddies, tiered plant stands, and other airy comforts. (C)

GARY BUXBAUM CO., LTD.
315 Hudson Street
New York, NY 10013
212-741-3899
Fine custom upholstery to the trade. (D)

GAZEBO OF NEW YORK
127 East 57 Street
New York, NY 10022
212-832-7077
Extensive country quilts, including custom, and other cozy country accessories. Chain. (C, R)

GIL ASSOCIATES
79 Bridge Street
Brooklyn, NY 11201
718-694-0272
Handmade, limited-production, contemporary children's wood furniture. Cabinets, rockers, and armchairs. (M, D)

GIRARD-EMILIA
200 Lexington Avenue
New York, NY 10016
212-679-4665
Fine reproductions of European antique carved-wood furniture, beautifully finished. (D)

GLASS TECH SERVICES, INC.
52-30 Van Dam Street
Long Island City, NY 11101
718-729-7000
Supplier and installer of Scotchtint window film. (I)

GROHE AMERICA, INC.
900 Lively Blvd.
Wood Dale, IL 60191
708-350-2600
Pull-out spray kitchen faucets with interchangeable heads for different functions (vegetable scrubbing, pots, etc.). (M)

HAMMACHER SCHLEMMER
147 East 57 Street
New York, NY 10022
212-421-9000
Specialty shop for convenience products throughout the house. (C, R)

HAND MADE QUILTS
PO Box 145
Lampeter, PA 17537
717-464-4598
Custom-made handworked Amish and patchwork quilts using customer's fabrics. (C)

HARDEN FURNITURE COMPANY
One Mill Pond Way
McConnellsville, NY 13401
315-245-1000
Quality reproduction Fine Traditional wood furniture. (M)

HASTINGS TILE & IL BAGNO
230 Park Avenue South
New York, NY 10003
212-674-9700
Upscale bath fixtures, including round showers, whirlpool tubs with back- and armrests, and steam showers. May be combined with fabulous custom tile applications. (M)

HEAT-N-GLO
6665 West Highway 13
Savage, MN 55378
800-669-HEAT
Direct-vented remote-control gas fireplaces. (M)

HERMAN MILLER, INC.
855 East Main Avenue
Zeeland, MI 49464-0302
616-654-8222
Classic Eames lounge chair and ottoman designed in 1956 by Charles and Ray Eames in leather upholstery and molded wood frames. (M)

HINSON CO.
27-35 Jackson Avenue
Long Island City, NY 11101-2917
212-475-4100
The original Hansen swing-arm lamps, available in chrome or brass finish with a variety of shades. (D)

HOLD EVERYTHING
PO Box 7807
San Francisco, CA 94120-7807
415-421-4242
Accessories for storage solutions, including coordinated closet garment bags and boxes. Chain. (C, R)

HOME DEPOT
2727 Paces Ferry Road
Atlanta, GA 30359
404-433-8211
800-553-3199
Leading-edge home-center store resource for contractors and do-it-yourselfers. Specialize in remodeling products. Personalized computer design for kitchen and bath. Chain. (R)

HONEYWELL, INC
1985 Douglas Drive N
Golden Valley, MN 55422
800-345-6770, Ext. 2039
Total home remote phone or panel heat, light, appliance, and security control systems. (M)

HUNTER FAN CO.
2500 Frisco Avenue
Memphis, TN 38114
901-743-1360
Ceiling fans and fan/light combinations. (M)

HUNTER-DOUGLAS
2 Park Way & Route 17 S
Upper Saddle River, NJ 07458
800-631-7274
Window shades, including Duette
micropleated fabric, Duette Eclipse for
total blackout. (M)

IPF INTERNATIONAL, INC.
Box 905
Paterson, NJ 07470
201-345-7740
From carved French to classic
Barcelona chair and ottoman. (D, M)

IAN HARRINGTON
298 East Montauk Highway
Southampton, NY 11968
516-728-0119
Anglo Raj furniture. Elegant and comfortable antique plantation furniture made
in India for English colonials. By appointment. (R)

INTERFORM
200 Lexington Avenue
New York, NY 10016
212-685-4959
Contemporary furniture, including
round dining table with foldout leaves. (D)

JACUZZI WHIRLPOOL BATH
100 N. Wiget Lane, PO Box J
Walnut Creek, CA 94596
800-678-6889
Spa-whirlpool water jet systems for
bathing and water massage. (M)

JEFFREY ARONOFF, INC.
16 West 23 Street, 3rd Floor
New York, NY 10010
212-645-3155
Sumptuous handwoven throws and
shawls. By appointment. (A)

JENN-AIR COMPANY
3035 Shadeland
Indianapolis, IN 46226-0901
317-545-2271
Cooktops with features such as
retractable ventilators and solid electric elements. (M)

JOANN AMOS
611 Bancumbe Street
Edgefield, SC 29824
803-637-2208
Decorative artist for faux finishes and
floor cloths. (A)

JOANNA WESTERN MILLS CO.
2141 S. Jefferson Street
Chicago, IL 60616
312-266-3232
1-800-562-6620
Wood blinds and shutters. (M)

JOHN P. MEYER & SONS
2645 Reeve Road
Mattituck, NY 11952
516-298-3882
General contractor for total renovation.
(A)

JOHN ROSSELLI
523 East 73 Street
New York, NY 10021
212-737-2252
Antiques and Niermann Weeks fine
reproductions. (R)

JOHN WIDDICOMB
601 Fifth Street NW
Grand Rapids, MI 49504
616-459-7173
Extensive collection of reproductions of
splendid antiques, including the Mario
Buatta collection of country English furniture with its classic Spencer chair and
ottoman. (M)

JOSEPH BIUNNO
129 West 29 Street
New York, NY 10016
212-629-5630
Decorative drapery hardware in period styling. (D)

JUVENILE LIFESTYLES, INC.
541 Eighth Street
San Francisco, CA 94103
800-WOW-4KID
Manufacturer of "Knight's Rest," a medieval castle bunk bed. (D)

KWC/WSWC
1559 Sunland Lane
Costa Mesa, CA 92626
714-557-1933
Scald-Gard faucets with retractable hand sprays for kitchen and bath, pressure balanced to maintain even heat. (M)

KOHLER CO.
Dept. A90
Kohler, WI 53044
800-4-KOHLER
State-of-the-art bath and kitchen fixtures and hardware, including the award-winning Precedence bath whirlpool equipped with a door that swings inward for easy access. (M)

KRAFT
306 East 61 Street
New York, NY 10021
212-838-2214
Broad variety of decorative hardware for selecting a comfortable look and feel. (D)

L. & J. G. STICKLEY, INC.
PO Box 480
Manlius, NY 13104-0480
315-682-5500
Faithful restatements and reproductions of original Stickley Mission Oak furniture with warm wood finishes and earthy-style comfort. (C)

LA BARGE
Holland, MI 49422
800-253-3870
Traditionally styled brass and glass furnishings, including mirrors, tea carts, and "go anywhere" tables. (M)

LANE FURNITURE COMPANY
PO Box 151
Altavista, VA 24517
804-369-5641
American West and Southwest furniture reproductions as well as many other styles for easy living. (M)

LA-Z-BOY CHAIR CO.
1284 N. Telegraph
Monroe, MI 48161
312-242-1444
Motion furniture, upholstered chairs, sofas, and sleep sofas. Executive reclining chair for desk. (M)

LAURA ASHLEY
714 Madison Avenue
New York, NY 10021
212-735-5000
English country fabrics, wallpapers, borders, and coordinated linens and accessories. Chain (R)

LERÓN
750 Madison Avenue
New York, NY 10021
212-753-6700
Exquisite luxury bedclothing. (R)

LIFE FITNESS, INC.
9601 Jeronimo Road
Irvine, CA 92718
800-735-3867
LifeCycle stationary bicycles. Fine service record. (M)

Ligne Roset
200 Lexington Avenue
New York, NY 10016
212-685-1099
Award-winning contemporary furniture by Europe's leading designers. Wonderfully imaginative convertible sofas, beds, tables, and chairs. (M)

Lorraine Furniture Co.
1460 Southlawn Lane
Rockville, MD 20850
301-340-8002
Wood-framed headboards with slip-out padded panels for instant reupholstering and ease of maintenance. (M)

Lun On Company
2565 Third Street, #329
San Francisco, CA 94107
415-550-7778
Matchstick bamboo blinds. (M)

Magic Chef
740 King Edward Avenue
Cleveland, TN 37311
615-472-3371
Electric smooth-top cooktop ranges and oven/range combinations. (M)

Martex
1185 Avenue of the Americas
New York, NY 10036
800-533-8229
Popular-priced bed and bath linens by renowned designers and architects, widely available in department stores. (M)

Marvin Windows
Box 100
Warroad, MN 56763
800-346-5128
Remote-control windows that open, close, and lock via a handheld or wall-panel programmable remote control. (M)

Masterworks
Box M, Dept. 68
Marietta, GA 30061
800-365-3555
Country charm lamps, prints, architectural accessories, and bent-willow headboards. (C)

Medina Decorators, Inc.
49 Lincoln Blvd.
Hempstead, NY 11550
516-481-4886
Custom shades, curtains, draperies, and coordinated carpet. (I)

Morton Books
989 Third Avenue
New York, NY 10022
212-421-9025
Everything you wanted to know about interior design and more! (R)

Mr. Steam
43-20 34 Street
Long Island City, NY 11101
718-937-4500
Personal steambath unit for installation in shower. (M)

Murphy Door Bed Co.
5300 New Horizons Blvd.
Amityville, NY 11701
516-957-5200
Makers of the original Murphy bed, which "disappears" into cabinets or walls. (M)

Museum of Modern Art Design Store
44 West 53 Street
New York, NY 10019
212-708-9700
Museum reproductions of modern furniture classics, accessories, and portable furniture. (C, R)

NANIK

PO Box 1766
Wausau, WI 54401
715-843-4900

Lexan vertical and horizontal blinds for privacy and glare reduction. May be motorized. (M)

NEWEL ART GALLERIES, INC.

425 East 53 Street
New York, NY 10022
212-758-1970

Array of fantasy antique furniture, including unique and delightful beds and recamiers. (D, R)

NIERMANN WEEKS COMPANY

2152 Renard Court
Annapolis, MD 21401
301-224-0133

Metal furniture of extraordinary craftsmanship and hand-painted Old World reproductions. (M)

NORDICTRACK

104 Peavey Road
Chaska, MN 55318
800-445-2360

NordicFlex Gold home gyms. (M)

NORSK, INC.

114 East 57 Street
New York, NY 10021
212-752-3111

Scandinavian furniture, including the body-friendly Stressless chair, the Mobilo reclining rocker, and adjustable rolling reading table. (R)

NORTH SHORE WEAVERS

347 Scudder Avenue
Northport, NY 11768
516-261-1818

Weavers of gorgeous custom colored throws. By appointment. (A)

NOUVEL SPACE

3850 Hardee Road
Coconut Grove, FL 33133
305-663-0011

Designs, supplies, and installs custom entertainment systems. (I)

OLD TOWN CROSSING

82 Main Street
Southampton, NY 11968
516-283-7740

Carefully selected English antiques, including comfortable upholstered pieces and exquisite accessories. (R)

ORCHID ISLAND TRADING CO.

Ocean Drive
Vero Beach, FL 32963
407-231-0620

For balmy southeastern Regional Flair, handmade sand sculptures, verdigris wood chimes, wicker birdcages, shaggy pastel rag rugs. (R)

PML FURNITURE GROUP

257 Park Avenue South
New York, NY 10010
212- 387-7922

Upscale office furniture and ergonomic chairs, including Vecta brand. (D)

PACE COLLECTION

11-11 34 Avenue
Long Island City, NY 11106
718-721-8201

Cushy, highly comfortable contemporary upholstered seating and stunning executive furniture. (M)

PALACEK

PO Box 225, Sta. A
Richmond, CA 94808-0225
800-227-2538

Wicker in Nantucket chaise, Bistro rocker, Cape Cod club chair, and other styles for rustic comfort. (M)

PALAZZETTI
215 Lexington Avenue
New York, NY 10016
212-684-1199
"The classics of modern furniture."
Reproductions of original prototypes,
including chaise lounges by Le Corbusier
and Mies van der Rohe, handsome serving
carts by Alvar Aalto. Chain. (R)

PATRICK CLARK
117-07 Beach Channel Drive
Rockaway Park, NY 11694-2010
718-474-2543
Master glassman and stained-glass artist
for doors, windows, and folding screens.
(A)

PAUL ASSOCIATES
155 East 55 Street
New York, NY 10022
212-755-1313
Luxurious contemporary plumbing fittings, hardware, and bath accessories,
including heated towel bars. (D)

PEA RIDGE PURITIES
311 East Washington Street
Fayetteville, TN 37334
615-433-0855
Handmade quilts, country crafts, and
accessories. (A, C)

PERIOD DETAILS, INC.
3516 Cadieux Road
Detroit, MI 48228
313-885-9237
Decorative painting for interiors and
furniture. Workshops available. (A)

PHIFER WIRE PRODUCTS
PO Box 1700
Tuscaloosa, AL 35403
800-633-5955
SunScreen and SheerWeave weather-
resistant fabrics for awnings and canopies.
(M)

PHOENIX SYSTEMS
3351 El Camino Real
Atherton, CA 94027
415-367-7100
Designs, supplies and installs state-of-
the-art home-entertainment systems,
including home theaters and multiroom
remote-control audio systems. (I)

PILLOW FINERY
979 Third Avenue, Suite 400
New York, NY 10022
212-752-9603
Pillows made to order in custom colors
and sizes. (D)

PIR IMPORTS
3033 N. Lincoln Avenue
Chicago, IL 60657
800-621-1244
Modestly priced reproduction European tapestries and Oriental rugs. (C)

PITTSBURGH CORNING CORP.
800 Presque Isle Drive
Pittsburgh, PA 15239
800-992-5769
Glass-block wall systems for indoor and
outdoor applications. (M)

PLAY MASTER-RENAISSANCE
PO Box 359
Bland, MO 65014
800-646-3294
Handcrafted billiard tables. (R)

POLO RALPH LAUREN
650 Madison Avenue
New York, NY 10022
212-318-7000
Well-designed and coordinated bed
linens, blankets, and luscious cashmere
throws. Chain. (M, R)

PORCELANOSA
1842 E. Jericho Turnpike
Dix Hills, NY 11746
516-462-6222
Outstanding European tiles for floors,
walls, and counters. Also in Anaheim, CA
(714) 772-3183. (M, R)

POYNOR GROUP
444 East 82 Street
New York, NY 10028
212-734-5909
　　Custom-designed and painted window shades. (A)

PRATESI
324 Worth Avenue
Palm Beach, FL 33480
407-655-4414
　　Premier bed linens in Fine Traditional styling. Also in Manhattan; Chicago; Washington, DC; Beverly Hills. (R)

PURE PODUNK, INC.
Old Schoolhouse Center, Box 194
Sharon, VT 05065
800-P-PODUNK
　　Natural organic pillows, mattresses, rugs, linens, and unfinished hardwood furniture for chemically sensitive or environmentally aware customers. (C)

QUIK-TRAK, INC.
84 Reservoir Park Drive
Rockland, MA 02370
800-872-8725
　　A system for mounting fabrics on everything for home decorating, including walls, ceilings, and headboards. (M)

QUOGUE EMPORIUM
98 Riverhead Road
Westhampton Beach, NY 11978
800-794-4438
　　White wicker, white lace, seashells, and a myriad other delightful "Hamptons" accessories. (R)

RELIABLE HOME OFFICE
PO Box 804117
Chicago, IL 60680-9968
800-869-6000
　　Office supplies and furnishings, including Incliner computer cart. (C)

REVOX AMERICA, INC.
1425 Elm Hill Pike
Nashville, TN 37210
615-254-5651
　　Duetto stereo speakers, a sound-state-quality speaker in a small triangular shape, which produces three-dimensional sound. (M)

RITTER ANTIK
1166 Second Avenue
New York, NY 10021
212-644-7442
　　Antique Continental neoclassical furniture, especially Biedermeier and Empire. (R)

ROLOKE CO.
5760 Hannum Avenue
Culver City, CA 90230
310-649-1807
　　Wal-Pil-O 4-in-1 specialty therapeutic neck pillows, wedges, and back supports. (M)

RUE DE FRANCE
78 Thames Street, Dept. PD
Newport RI 02840
401-846-2084
　　Lovely lace panels for windows and doors. Swathe beds! (C)

S. T. PRESTON & SON, INC.
102 Main Street
Greenport, NY 11944
516-477-1990
　　Nautical-themed accessories for the home with New England regional flair. (R)

SAUDER WOODWORKING
502 Middle Street
Archbold, OH 43502
800-537-8560
　　Home office furniture and wall entertainment units, modestly priced. (M)

SCALAMANDRÉ
950 Third Avenue
New York, NY 10022
212-467-8800
Beautiful assortment of fine French fabrics, including historic reproductions. (D)

SCANDIA DOWN
455 Park Plaza Drive
LaCrosse, WI 54601
800-237-5337
European goose-down comforters and pillows. (C)

SEALY, INC.
1228 Euclid Avenue
Cleveland, OH 44115-1888
216-522-1310
Bedding, water beds, sleep sofas. (M)

SEARS & SEARS
Beach Lane, Box 917
Quogue, NY 11959
516-653-4218
Outstanding architect for remodeling or planning new homes of extraordinary comfort. (A)

SEATUCK ELECTRIC CO.
PO Box 523
Speonk, NY 11972
516-325-1371
Electrical contractor. (I)

SELECT COMFORT SLEEP SYSTEMS
11010 89 Avenue N
Maple Grove, MN 55369
800-831-1211
Unique air-support system allows for dual independent control of mattress firmness—one side can be softer than the other. (C, M)

SENTIMENTO
306 East 61 Street
New York, NY 10021
212-750-3111
Delightful "smalls," exquisite antique accessories for the desk, vanity, and bar. (R, D)

SEVENTH GENERATION
Colchester, VT 05446-1672
800-456-1177
Ecologically sound cleaners, recyclers, bedding, storage, and reuse items. (C)

SHANNON & JEAL
188 Illinois Street
San Francisco, CA 94124
415-641-9444
Magnificently sculptured iron four-posters, canopy frames, headboards, and daybeds. (M)

SHARP ELECTRONICS CORP.
Sharp Plaza
Mahwah, NJ 07430-2135
201-529-8200
Electronics manufacturer, including full-scale copier/fax combination. (M)

SHARPER IMAGE
650 Davis Street
San Francisco, CA 94111
800-344-4444
Heated towel racks, First Edition exercise equipment, among others, AcuMassage table, and motorized recliner with built-in massage and stereo. Chain. (C)

SHYAM AHUJA
201 East 56 Street
New York, NY 10022
212-644-5910
Cotton, woven, and crewel area rugs. (M)

SIEDLE
750 Parkway
Broomall, PA 19008
800-874-3353
215-353-9595
"Intelligent" intercom systems for controlling security, lighting, and gates. (M)

SMITH & HAWKEN
25 Corte Madera
Mill Valley, CA 94941
415-383-2000
Pawleys Island rope hammocks, courting swings, market umbrellas, water hyacinth hammocks, steamer chairs, and other delicious airy comforts. (C)

SOFT BATHTUB CO.
10711 Cambie Road, Suite 272
Richmond, British Columbia V6X3G5
    CAN
800-882-7638
604-244-7638
Tub with revolutionary top layer that's cushiony yet tough, retains heat, is easy to clean, and allows sure footing. Cushioned comfort in many colors. (M)

SOLAR SCREEN
53-11 105 Street
Corona, NY 11368
718-592-8222
KoolVue window shades. Translucent, one-way-view plastic-film roller shades. (M)

SOMFY SYSTEMS, INC.
2 Sutton Place
Edison, NJ 08817
800-22-SOMFY
Fingertip control for retractable awnings. Sun and wind sensors work automatically to protect from heat and rain. (M)

SOUND ADVANCE SYSTEMS
3202 South Shannon Street
Santa Ana, CA 92704-6353
800-892-9002
High-performance speaker that is invisible when installed. (M)

SOUTHWEST GALLERY
550-04 North Country Road
St. James, NY 11780
516-862- 6127
Authentic southwestern furniture, pottery and artwork. (R)

SPEAKMAN
PO Box 191
Wilmington, DE 19899-0191
302-764-9100
Sensorflo electronic touchless faucets for kitchen, baths, and powder rooms. (M)

STAIRMASTER
610 N. Xathus
Tulsa, OK 74130
800-331-3578
Easy-to-use stair climber for cardiovascular and lower-body fitness. (M)

STAPLES
1075 Avenue of the Americas
New York, NY 10036
800-333-3330
Discount office supplies and machinery. (C)

STARK CARPETS
979 Third Avenue
New York, NY 10022
212-752-9000
Specialists in custom colorations and design. Carries a wealth of quality carpets and rugs. (D)

STARK LOBSTER & MARINE SYSTEMS
29-14 122 Street
College Point, NY 11354
718-445-5357
Spectacular large-sized marine aquariums with automatic filtering systems requiring no change of water.

STUDIO EAST EXERCISE CENTER
at Hampton Square, Box 1148
Westhampton Beach, NY 11978
516-288-1273
Fitness consultant will design home gym. (A)

TERRY L. MORTON
146 East 84 Street
New York, NY 10028
212-472-1446
Creator of pricey antique tapestry, needlepoint, and other exquisite pillows. By appointment. (A)

THANK HEAVEN FOR LITTLE ONES
PO Box 707
Buchanan, VA 24066
703-254-1780
Whimsical children's furniture, ranging from the Heirloom Look to Brad's House, decorated with artistic kids' graffiti. (M, D)

THIEF RIVER LINENS
502 N. David Avenue
Thief River Falls, MN 56701
218-681-3919
Highly styled custom linens using imported fabrics in unusual hues. Marvelous pillows! (M)

THIMBELINA
123 Stephen Hands Path
East Hampton, NY 11937
516-324-0729
Mario Buatta needlepoint pillows. (M)

THOMAS P. RICHMOND, INC.
79 Longview Avenue
White Plains, NY 10605
914- 428-2511
Lighting consultant for interior and exterior lighting design, including projector lights. (I)

THONET INDUSTRIES
403 Meachan Road
Statesville, NC 28687
800-551-6702
Classic bentwood rocker designed by Michael Thonet, continuously popular since its introduction in 1862. (M)

3M ENERGY CONTROL PRODUCTS
225-4S-08, 3M Center
St. Paul, MN 55144-1000
Scotchtint sun-control film to reduce glare and increase heating/cooling efficiency. See Yellow Pages, "Glass Coating." (M)

TREADLES, N.Y.
95 Horatio Street
New York, NY 10014
212-633-0072
Fine handwoven textiles and throws in a vast array of patterns and materials. (M)

TRICONFORT
200 Lexington Avenue
New York, NY 10022
212-685-7035
Terrific weatherproof indoor/outdoor wicker.

TROPITONE FURNITURE CO.
PO Box 3197
Sarasota, FL 34230
813-355-2692
Patio furnishings, including gliders, rockers, and swivel chairs for relaxed airy comforts. (M)

TROTTER
Ten Trotter Drive
Medway, MA 02053
800-677-6544
Excellent treadmill for home gym. Outstanding customer service for maintenance and repairs. (M)

ULTRASUEDE
104 West 40 Street
New York, NY 10018
212-556-6500
Durable, washable, stain-resistant, colorfast man-made suede in dozens of colors. For upholstery. (M)

UPSTAIRS DOWN SHOP
1005 Madison Avenue
New York, NY 10021
212-861-7000
   European down comforters. (C, R)

UTICA
1185 Avenue of the Americas
New York, NY 10036
800-533-8229
   Bed and bath linens, including overscale
towels for drying comfort. Pure cotton,
chemical free towels and sheet sets. Available in department stores. (M)

VECTA
1800 S. Great Southwest Place
Grand Prairie, TX 75051
214-641-2860
   Upscale ergonomic office chairs. (M)

VERMONT CASTINGS
Route 107, Box 501
Bethel, VT 05032
802-234-2330
   EPA-approved glass-enameled wood-
stoves. (M)

VERMONT TEDDY BEAR CO.
2031 Shelburne Road
Shelburne, VT 05482
800-829-BEAR
   Handcrafted, washable, comforting
bears shipped direct for all occasions. (C)

VESTA INC.
801 East River Street
Anderson, SC 29624
803-225-8054
1-800-638-3782
   Decorative drapery rods and accessories, including Louis XV/XVI, Anglais,
Empire, 1930s style. (M)

WAVERLY, INC.
79 Madison Avenue
New York, NY 10036
212-213-8100
   Well-priced, good-looking fabrics with
coordinating wallpapers and borders. (M)

WHITE HOME PRODUCTS, INC.
2401 Lake Park Drive
Atlanta, GA 30080
404-431-0900
   Closet carousels and movable storage
systems. (M)

WILLIAMS-SONOMA
5750 Hollis Street
Emoryville, CA 94608
415-652-1553
   Comfortable cooking and serving accessories. Chain. (C, R)

WILLIAMSBURG REPRODUCTIONS
Craft House
Williamsburg, VA 23185
800-446-9240
   Authentic fine Colonial reproductions
of the famed museum's furniture and accessories, including sheltering wing chairs
(300-page color catalog).

WINDOW MODES/MODERN
WINDOW
979 Third Avenue
New York, NY 10022
212-752-1140
   Motorized vertical blinds and awnings,
Roman shades; balloon curtains, string
draperies. (D, I)

WINTERTHUR MUSEUM & GARDENS
Winterthur, DE 19736
   Excellent reproductions of antique fur-
nishings, licensed by the museum and car-
rying the Winterthur trademark.
(C, R)

WOODSTOCK SOAPSTONE CO.,
INC.
Airpark Road, Box 37H/211
West Lebanon, NH 03784
800-866-4344
   Patented in 1797, these handcrafted
woodstoves have been warming New Eng-
land homes for over a century. (M, R)

YAMAHA CORPORATION OF
AMERICA
PO Box 6600
Buena Park, CA 90622
800-648-2845
    "Disklavier" disc-driven player piano.
(M)

YANKEE PRIDE
29 Parkside Circle, Dept. L13
Braintree, MA 02184
617-848-7610
    Braided, hooked, and rag rugs. (C)

ZONA
97 Greene Street
New York, NY 10003
212-925-6750
    American West accessories in metal,
wood, leather, and glass. (R)

About the Authors

Teri Seidman, President of Teri Seidman Interiors of New York City and Westhampton Beach, has been designing since 1975 and is best known for her sophisticated town and country interiors. Her work received first place in an American Society of Interior Designers national interior design competition. Lecturer and a contributing editor of *House: Lifestyle of the Island,* Seidman's work is frequently featured in designer show houses as well as in many international publications (including *HG, Hong Kong Journal, Country Decorating, Woman's Day,* and *The New York Times*) as well as on CNN's *Style* program. She is an Allied Member of ASID, a member of IFDA, the Allied Board of Trade, and the Fashion Group.

She and coauthor Sherry Suib Cohen wrote the Book-of-the-Month-Club's bestselling *Decorating Rich: How to Achieve a Monied Look Without Spending a Fortune* (Villard, 1988).

Sherry Suib Cohen is the author of *Secrets of a Very Good Marriage: Lessons from the Sea* (Carol Southern Books/Crown, 1993), and thirteen other books.

She is a contributing editor of *New Woman,* and is regularly published in many other national magazines including *Brides and Your New Home, Family Circle, Ladies' Home Journal, Glamour, Woman's Day, Redbook,* and *Mirabella.* She lectures nationwide and often appears on radio and television shows such as *Oprah, Donahue, Good Day New York,* and *Sally Jessy Raphael,* to talk about her work.

She is a former board member of the American Society of Journalists and Authors.